TO LIVE IS CHRIST TO DIE IS GAIN

D0823964

MATT CHANDLER

Published by

3405 Milton Avenue, Suite 207
Dallas, TX 75205

Printed in the United States

RESOURCES

Ecclesiastes

A Life Well Lived (A Study of Ecclesiastes)
Bible Study Series by Tommy Nelson
> 4 DVD Curriculum
> Companion Study Guide
> A Life Well Lived paperback book

The Mingling of Souls

NEW! A Study of Attraction, Love, Marriage & Redemption from Song of Solomon
Bible Study Series by Matt Chandler
> 2 DVD Curriculum
> Companion Study Guide
> Packages and bulk discounts available

Romans

Romans, The Letter that Changed the World, Vol. I and II
Bible Study Series by Tommy Nelson
> DVD Curriculum
> Companion Study Guide
> Packages and bulk discounts available

Ruth

NEW! Ruth; Your God, My God. A True Story of Love & Redemption
Bible Study Series by Tommy Nelson
> 4 DVD Curriculum
> Companion Study Guide
> Packages and bulk discounts available

Song of Solomon

NEW and Improved! 1995 Song of Solomon Classic
DVD Curriculum by Tommy Nelson
> Enhanced video, audio and color graphics
> Updated and enlarged companion Study Guide
> Formatted for Widescreen

NEW! Enhanced SOS for Students
DVD Curriculum by Tommy Nelson
> Re-Mastered Video & Audio
> All new graphics and menus
> Never before seen Q & A's
> All in one Study Guide for both Students & Leaders

Vintage Jesus

Vintage Jesus, Timeless Answers to Timely Questions
Bible Study Series by Mark Driscoll
> 4 DVD Curriculum
> Companion Study Guide
> Packages and bulk discounts available

ACKNOWLEDGEMENTS

The Hub wants to thank the following friends, without whose help, this series and study guide would not have been possible:

Jim Gribnitz, Crosswise Media (Study Guide Consultant and Behind the Book) • **Chris Chavez,** Associate to Matt Chandler at The Village Church • **Amazing studio recording audience and friends** at The Village Church • **Matt Coleman,** Unblind Productions, Producer • **Drew Rodgers,** Livingstone Designs • **Shatrine Krake,** Krake Designs • **Sue Ann Reynolds,** Round Tu-it Office Support • **Jason Countryman,** PocketPak Albums • **John Dempsey and PCS Productions,** Lighting • **Matt Chandler,** Pastor, The Village Church, Dallas, TX

The Amazing views of Downtown Dallas provided by:
This study was filmed at the beautiful and exclusive homes of The Azure in downtown Dallas. For information on The Azure you can visit www.azureliving.com.

The Hub wishes to thank **Harwood International** (www.harwoodinternational.com/azure.php) **and the entire staff at The Azure.** The views you have are the best in the city and the spirit of the team was fantastic. Thanks again for your hospitality.

Lastly we thank **David C Cook** in their partnership with this project and allowing us to utilize the graphics and cover of their release of the trade book by Matt Chandler on his teaching of Philippians. Thank you **David C Cook.**

ABOUT THE HUB

Thanks for taking a moment to learn more about us. Our organization began in 1995 working with one speaker, Tommy Nelson and one amazing message, The Song of Solomon. It was and is our privilege to help champion God's written Word on Love, Dating, Marriage and Sex based directly on Song of Solomon. It is a book that has been censored for centuries and it has been a total blessing and thrill to see it change my life, and millions of others.

As of August 2009 we have rebranded our organization to reflect the root of our passion and the future of our organization:

To Develop, Find and Share life changing Bible Centric tools that move people forward. We have renamed our organization to The Hub. It is our passion and commitment to be a Hub for unique, challenging and grace filled resources. I hope you will agree after you participate and interact with one of our resources.

God Bless you and know that if you will listen, God's Truth will move you forward in life, no matter where you have been or are currently.

Doug Hudson, *President - The Hub*

TABLE OF CONTENTS

STUDY TIPS

BEFORE YOU GO ANY FURTHER... READ THIS!

If you are a small group leader, thanks for taking the opportunity to shepherd others along the way. And if you are using this series for personal study, get ready for a life-changing experience you will want to share with others! Here are a few tips as you get started with the series:

- This study was designed with small groups in mind. So put a small group together and get started.
- The series is also perfect for individuals or couples who are looking for ways to deepen their devotions or find practical ways to apply the timeless truths of Scripture.
- Philippians is designed to be used as either a 12-week or a 6-week study. Each DVD session is approximately 30 minutes. The sessions are designed to be used as follows: watch each session and then discuss the questions in the Study Guide.
- Depending on the length of your meeting time, you can watch two sessions per meeting to make Philippians a 6-week series.

A WORD TO SMALL GROUP LEADERS

Special Note - take a moment to go to **Behind The Book** feature (page 85). This is a quick overview that will give you the who, what, when, where and why of Philippians.

There is no separate leader's guide. Leaders are facilitators of the material: Answers to Text Questions are in the back of Study Guide.

Before each session we encourage leaders to:

- **Pray** – ask the Lord for guidance on how to lead the members in your group. Pray that He will show you ways to stimulate genuine, dynamic and open communication.
- **Preview** – it will be very beneficial for you to watch the session before you share it with your group. You will notice the key points from each session and you can better facilitate the discussion questions within your group.
- **Prepare** – a small group will only go as deep and be as transparent as the leader. If a leader or facilitator is not willing to get personal, then the group will float on the surface. Let God speak through your own struggles and weaknesses.

ABOUT THE AUTHOR

Matt Chandler serves as Lead Pastor of The Village Church in Dallas, TX. He describes his tenure since 2002 at The Village as a re-planting effort where he was involved in changing the theological and philosophical culture of the congregation.

The church has witnessed a tremendous response growing from 160 people to over 10,000 including satellite campuses in Dallas and Denton. In March of 2012, Matt was named president of Acts 29 Network, which is a network of over 400 churches in the United States and abroad planting church-planting churches. Matt authored *The Explicit Gospel*, to remind us what is of first and utmost importance – the Gospel. It is call to true Christianity, to know the Gospel explicitly and to unite the church on the amazing grounds of the good news of Jesus.

His greatest joy outside of Jesus is being married to Lauren and being a dad to their three children, Audrey, Reid and Norah.

INTRODUCTION

If someone has read only one book of the Bible, often I find it to be Philippians.

Paul's letter to the Philippians is one of the most taught books of the Bible from the pulpit today and with excellent reason. The book is simple, straightforward, and broadly relevant—easy for all Christians to understand and apply.

Often people come away from this text and sum it up in one word: 'joy'. This is both true and tragic.

It is true in the sense that the letter is conceivably the quintessential treatise on joy that all believers must read to see the fullness of joy with which Christians are intended to live. The letter makes joy real, practical, and alive and is unmistakably a vital part of this great text.

But it is also tragic to sum it up simply as 'joy', in that there is so much more there. It answers all sorts of practical questions for the believer today:

- How can I effectively share my faith?
- What does it mean to live a worthy Christian life?
- What does true Christian humility look like?
- Where can I find true satisfaction for my soul?
- How can I rejoice during tragedy?
- What do I do when I am stressed?
- What does a passionate follower of Christ look like?

Not only does this letter answer many questions for the believer - it also paints a beautiful picture of what the mature Christian life is.

Enjoy this expositional teaching of Philippians—a book you may have heard many times—like you have never heard it before.

ODD BEGINNINGS

ACTS 16:6-40

Ironically, in this study of Paul's letter to the Philippians, we ask you first to open your Bible to... not Philippians. We start out this study of Philippians in the 16th chapter of the book of Acts. Allow me to illustrate why that would be.

Though I am not as avid a world-traveler as many, I have been on numerous national and international mission trips. When I get back home, I generally tell my friends and family only a little bit about the culture, the sights, the accommodations, and the travel itself, but I spend the majority of my time talking to anyone that will listen about the people. My photo albums are not filled with pictures of the (often breathtaking) scenery, but I have scores of pictures of the people that I met while serving there. The individuals in the area are the reason I went in the first place. They are the topics that consume my post-trip conversations and memories which I will keep with me for life.

The most important thing about the mission trip is the people. It is the people that endear the city to our heart. The same is true for Paul and the Philippians.

On Paul's second missionary journey (recorded in Acts 16), he spends time in Philippi. It is this experience in Philippi that sets the backdrop for the letter that he would write later to the Philippians. Before we study that letter we need to meet the people that Paul met. This first session introduces us to three people that Paul met in Philippi whose stories the Scriptures have preserved for us to study for centuries. Their stories and backgrounds could not possibly be any different.

Though every church has a somewhat unique story of its beginnings, none is as unique as Philippi, the first church in the history of all of Europe. The story is far from how you and I would start the Christian movement on a continent. But then, again, God is a touch smarter than we are.

The birth of the church in Philippi is truly an odd and seemingly unadvisable way to start a church, but isn't that just like God?

Let's check it out.

⁶And they went through the region of Phrygia and Galatia, having been forbidden by the Holy Spirit to speak the word in Asia. ⁷And when they had come up to Mysia, they attempted to go into Bithynia, but the Spirit of Jesus did not allow them. ⁸So, passing by Mysia, they went down to Troas. ⁹And a vision appeared to Paul in the night: a man of Macedonia was standing there, urging him and saying, "Come over to Macedonia and help us." ¹⁰And when Paul had seen the vision, immediately we sought to go on into Macedonia, concluding that God had called us to preach the gospel to them.

¹¹So, setting sail from Troas, we made a direct voyage to Samothrace, and the following day to Neapolis, ¹²and from there to Philippi, which is a leading city of the district of Macedonia and a Roman colony. We remained in this city some days. ¹³And on the Sabbath day we went outside the gate to the riverside, where we supposed there was a place of prayer, and we sat down and spoke to the women who had come together. ¹⁴One who heard us was a woman named Lydia, from the city of Thyatira, a seller of purple goods, who was a worshiper of God. The Lord opened her heart to pay attention to what was said by Paul. ¹⁵And after she was baptized, and her household as well, she urged us, saying, "If you have judged me to be faithful to the Lord, come to my house and stay." And she prevailed upon us.

¹⁶As we were going to the place of prayer, we were met by a slave girl who had a spirit of divination and brought her owners much gain by fortune-telling. ¹⁷She followed Paul and us, crying out, "These men are servants of the Most High God, who proclaim to you the way of salvation." ¹⁸And this she kept doing for many days. Paul, having become greatly annoyed, turned and said to the spirit, "I command you in the name of Jesus Christ to come out of her." And it came out that very hour.

19But when her owners saw that their hope of gain was gone, they seized Paul and Silas and dragged them into the marketplace before the rulers. 20And when they had brought them to the magistrates, they said, "These men are Jews, and they are disturbing our city. 21They advocate customs that are not lawful for us as Romans to accept or practice." 22The crowd joined in attacking them, and the magistrates tore the garments off them and gave orders to beat them with rods. 23And when they had inflicted many blows upon them, they threw them into prison, ordering the jailer to keep them safely. 24Having received this order, he put them into the inner prison and fastened their feet in the stocks.

25About midnight Paul and Silas were praying and singing hymns to God, and the prisoners were listening to them, 26and suddenly there was a great earthquake, so that the foundations of the prison were shaken. And immediately all the doors were opened, and everyone's bonds were unfastened. 27When the jailer woke and saw that the prison doors were open, he drew his sword and was about to kill himself, supposing that the prisoners had escaped. 28But Paul cried with a loud voice, "Do not harm yourself, for we are all here." 29And the jailer called for lights and rushed in, and trembling with fear he fell down before Paul and Silas. 30Then he brought them out and said, "Sirs, what must I do to be saved?" 31And they said, "Believe in the Lord Jesus, and you will be saved, you and your household." 32And they spoke the word of the Lord to him and to all who were in his house. 33And he took them the same hour of the night and washed their wounds; and he was baptized at once, he and all his family. 34Then he brought them up into his house and set food before them. And he rejoiced along with his entire household that he had believed in God.

35But when it was day, the magistrates sent the police, saying, "Let those men go." 36And the jailer reported these words to Paul, saying, "The magistrates have sent to let you go. Therefore come out now and go in peace." [37]But Paul said to them, "They have beaten us publicly, uncondemned, men who are Roman citizens, and have thrown us into prison; and do they now throw us out secretly? No! Let them come themselves and take us out." [38]The police reported these words to the magistrates, and they were afraid when they heard that they were Roman citizens. [39]So they came and apologized to them. And they took them out and asked them to leave the city. [40]So they went out of the prison and visited Lydia. And when they had seen the brothers, they encouraged them and departed.

DISCUSSION QUESTIONS

1. *(Per the DVD)* What are the relation-ships you have into which you could bring the gospel? What reasons keep you from sharing it boldly?

_____

_____

_____

_____

_____

_____

_____

_____

_____

_____

IN ORDER TO UNDERSTAND THIS LETTER, YOU HAVE TO UNDERSTAND ITS BEGINNINGS.

2. Describe the people that Paul meets in Philippi as described in Acts 16 and how the gospel is shown or spoken to each of them:

A. Lydia (16:14-15)_____

_____

_____

B. The demon-possessed girl (16:16-18)_____

_____

_____

C. The Jailer (16:23-34)_____

_____

_____

3. Paul approached three different people three very different ways. What does that say about how we spread the good news today?

A. How would you approach a 'Lydia' today? Similar to how Paul did or differently?

B. Probably you do not regularly encounter demon-possessed girls in our culture today. Is there any modern-day application for the approach Paul took to the demon-possessed girl?

C. The conversion of the jailer is remarkable in that Paul was able to forgive his unnecessary stocks for the sake of telling him about Christ. Why could Paul forgive so quickly something so awful and undeserved, yet we are so slow to forgive wrongs done to us?

A._____

_____

_____

_____

B._____

_____

_____

C._____

_____

_____

DON'T JUST READ THE BIBLE. BE THERE. SMELL IT.

4. In the first two conversions, Paul approached the women with words. In the third (the jailer) he used only actions, and the man begged him to tell him about Jesus. What does this say about the balance of words and actions communicating the gospel in our culture today?

_____

_____

_____

_____

_____

_____

_____

5. Our goal is to help transform lives and help you understand the Bible better. Every session we will have you practice a great Bible study technique. We will ask that you summarize the teaching in a sentence. This helps remind you of what you learned and gives a tangible sense of what you read. Go ahead and do that now.

_____

_____

_____

_____

_____

_____

_____

_____

_____

_____

_____

_____

_____

IF YOU ARE HONEST, YOU WILL DO LIFE WITH PEOPLE WHO ARE SIMILAR TO YOU...THE THING THE GOSPEL DID HERE, IS THAT IT BLEW THROUGH ALL OF THAT AND CREATED A NEW COMMUNITY THAT WOULD HAVE NEVER TAKEN PLACE BEFORE IT HIT.

memory verse

Then the jailer brought them out and said, "Sirs, what must I do to be saved?" And they said, "Believe in the Lord Jesus, and you will be saved, you and your household." (Acts 16:30-31, ESV)

DIVING DEEPER

Map of Philippi with Paul's missionary journey.

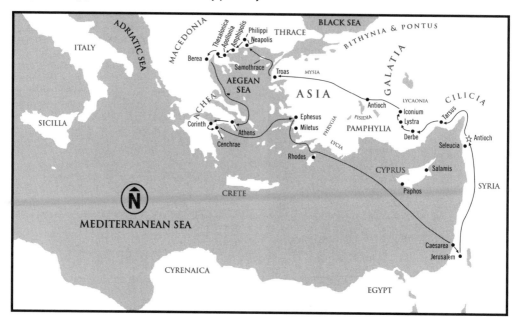

prayer requests

THE WORTHY LIFE 2

PHILIPPIANS 1:1-30

Employment evaluation with a supervisor is no one's favorite. It is difficult to sit down toe-to-toe with him or her and hear whether or not you have measured up to expectations. It is easier to simply assume everything is OK, focus on your personal strengths, and never have anyone point out your blind spots.

It is *easier*, but it is not *best*.

Every so often it is helpful as an employee to evaluate if you are worth what they are paying you. It is healthy and appropriate to determine: are you worth it? Are you worthy of the paycheck you are receiving? Are the actions and results you produce in your daily job, *worth* what you are being paid?

If we would be doing that for something as silly and temporary as a job, why wouldn't we do that with our faith? It should be a wonderful checkup for us to evaluate our lives, examine our hearts and see if we are living a life worthy of the gospel.

Are we? Let's find out.

¹Paul and Timothy, servants of Christ Jesus, To all the saints in Christ Jesus who are at Philippi, with the overseers and deacons: ²Grace to you and peace from God our Father and the Lord Jesus Christ.

³I thank my God in all my remembrance of you, ⁴always in every prayer of mine for you all making my prayer with joy, ⁵because of your partnership in the gospel from the first day until now. ⁶And I am sure of this, that he who began a good work in you will bring it to completion at the day of Jesus Christ. ⁷It is right for me to feel this way about you all, because I hold you in my heart, for you are all partakers with me of grace, both in my imprisonment and in the defense and confirmation of the gospel. ⁸For God is my witness, how I yearn for you all with the affection of Christ Jesus. ⁹And it is my prayer that your love may abound more and more, with knowledge and all discernment, ¹⁰so that you may approve what is excellent, and so be pure and blameless for the day of Christ, ¹¹filled with the fruit of righteousness that comes through Jesus Christ, to the glory and praise of God.

¹²I want you to know, brothers, that what has happened to me has really served to advance the gospel, ¹³so that it has become known throughout the whole imperial guard and to all the rest that my imprisonment is for Christ. ¹⁴And most of the brothers, having become confident in the Lord by my imprisonment, are much more bold to speak the word without fear.

¹⁵Some indeed preach Christ from envy and rivalry, but others from good will. ¹⁶The latter do it out of love, knowing that I am put here for the defense of the gospel. ¹⁷The former proclaim Christ out of rivalry, not sincerely but thinking to afflict me in my imprisonment. ¹⁸What then? Only that in every way, whether in pretense or in truth, Christ is proclaimed, and in that I rejoice.

Yes, and I will rejoice, [19]for I know that through your prayers and the help of the Spirit of Jesus Christ this will turn out for my deliverance, [20]as it is my eager expectation and hope that I will not be at all ashamed, but that with full courage now as always Christ will be honored in my body, whether by life or by death. [21]For to me to live is Christ, and to die is gain. [22]If I am to live in the flesh, that means fruitful labor for me. Yet which I shall choose I cannot tell. [23]I am hard pressed between the two. My desire is to depart and be with Christ, for that is far better. [24]But to remain in the flesh is more necessary on your account. [25]Convinced of this, I know that I will remain and continue with you all, for your progress and joy in the faith, [26]so that in me you may have ample cause to glory in Christ Jesus, because of my coming to you again.

[27]Only let your manner of life be worthy of the gospel of Christ, so that whether I come and see you or am absent, I may hear of you that you are standing firm in one spirit, with one mind striving side by side for the faith of the gospel, [28]and not frightened in anything by your opponents. This is a clear sign to them of their destruction, but of your salvation, and that from God. [29]For it has been granted to you that for the sake of Christ you should not only believe in him but also suffer for his sake, [30]engaged in the same conflict that you saw I had and now hear that I still have.

DISCUSSION QUESTIONS

1. *(Per the DVD)* If the mature Christian life is a life where you (A) do life deeply with others regardless of external differences, (B) strive for holiness, and (C) press into Christ in fearlessness, are you growing in your relationship?

A._____

_____

B._____

_____

C._____

_____

_____

_____

WHEN YOU TAKE A DOMINANT LEADER LIKE PAUL, AND YOU REMOVE HIM FROM A SETTING, WHAT ENDS UP HAPPENING IS OTHER PEOPLE START FILLING IN THAT GAP, THAT VACUUM.

2. Describe some of the difficulties and challenges to living a life worthy of the gospel in our culture today. Be specific!

_____

_____

_____

_____

_____

3. What impact does the dramatic polarization of our society (*i.e. Republican vs. Democrat, Christian vs. non-Christian, etc.*) have in your life? As you share the gospel? As you build relationships with others? What are some other polarized groups that affect you on a regular basis?

_____
_____
_____
_____
_____
_____
_____
_____
_____
_____
_____
_____
_____
_____
_____

PRISON IN THE FIRST CENTURY, I'M GUESSING, IS VERY DIFFERENT THAN IT IS TODAY. THEY DON'T HAVE CABLE, THEY DON'T HAVE OUTSIDE TIME, AND I'M PRETTY SURE NO ONE COMES ALONG CHECKING TO SEE IF YOU GET YOUR MEALS.

4.What are the barriers and external characteristics that we unconsciously (perhaps) use to divide our society and put people into different 'groups' in our minds?

_____
_____
_____
_____
_____
_____
_____
_____

5. List some of the factors and issues that keep Christians from standing together as one. How could this be improved among evangelicals?

LYDIA–THE SLAVE GIRL–THE JAILER. THEY WERE ALL SLAVES TO THESE WAYS OF LIFE THAT MEN AND WOMEN CHOOSE. PAUL HAD SEEN THE DYSFUNCTION IN IT AND THEN SEEN THE JOY THAT COMES WHEN THE GOSPEL OVERPOWERS IT. OF COURSE HE'S SAYING 'TO LIVE IS CHRIST'. THERE IS NO OPTION FOR HIM!

6. The Greek word for 'strive' in 1:27 is συναθλέω (synathleō). It is defined as: "work with someone, implying against an opposition or competitive struggle"[1] and is used only here and in Philippians 4:3. What does that verse and that definition imply about how we ought to 'strive'?

[1] James Swanson, *Dictionary of Biblical Languages With Semantic Domains : Greek (New Testament)*, electronic ed. (Oak Harbor: Logos Research Systems, Inc., 1997), DBLG 5254.

7. Agree or disagree: Most Christians strive in many areas of life except their faith.

A. If this is true, why is that and what can be done about it?

B. In what other areas do you strive?

8. Why do Christians erroneously think that when we come to faith, our daily sin should disappear more than it does in reality? Where did we get this idea?

A. Let's not make the same mistake. How can we communicate tension between the unacceptability of sinning for the Christian, and yet the reality that we will still sin?

9. Define: "Fearless Christianity" and explain why it is so hard to practice?

A._____

_____

_____

B._____

_____

_____

_____

_____

_____

A._____

_____

_____

_____

_____

_____

_____

_____

_____

_____

_____

10. Summarize the teaching of this passage in one sentence.

_____
_____
_____
_____
_____
_____
_____
_____
_____
_____
_____
_____

memory verse

Only let your manner of life be worthy of the gospel of Christ, so that whether I come and see you or am absent, I may hear of you, that you are standing firm in one spirit, with one mind, striving side by side for the faith of the gospel, and not frightened in anything by your opponents. This is a clear sign to them of their destruction, but of your salvation, and that from God. (Philippians 1:27-28, ESV)

For me to live is Christ, and to die is gain. (Philippians 1:21, ESV)

DIVING DEEPER

Paul had no fear of man, but a healthy 'fear' of God.

The Bible is replete with this concept. Go to your favorite online Bible and search the word 'fear' to see what it teaches on this topic.

Here are some starters:
>   Matthew 10:26-33
>   2 Timothy 1:7
>   1 John 4:18
>   Hebrews 13:1-6
>   Psalms 27:1, 118:6

Explore what the Bible teaches about fearing God vs. man.

prayer requests

_____

_____

_____

_____

_____

_____

_____

_____

_____

NOTES

THE ONE GOD EXALTS 3

PHILIPPIANS 2:1-4, LUKE 1:39-55

Matthew 18:23-35 gives us a picture of a man that owes the king ten thousand talents (a bunch). He could not repay it, so the king demanded that his wife and kids be sold until the debt was repaid! The servant fell and begged for patience so he could repay it and the king compassionately removed the debt from him. (Catch that—the man asked only for some time to pay it off, but the king cancelled the debt altogether!)

That same servant left that meeting with the king and went out and found one of his servants who owed him a hundred denarii (not much). He grabbed him, choked him, and the man begged asking for patience to repay. As he choked the man, he should have thought back to ten minutes ago when he asked the king the exact same thing for a much larger debt. What would his response be? Would he ooze mercy and forgiveness like the king did with his large debt? Nope. Instead, some of the most remarkably arrogant and ungrateful words ever uttered come out of his mouth.

"Pay what you owe."

How insane that the one who had just received mercy upon mercy for a large debt, now offers none for a much smaller one!

So it is with mercy and forgiveness, is it not? We have been forgiven greatly from God and He has, through the blood of Christ, taken our punishment for sin from us. We should be the most humble, merciful, forgiving people on the planet, right? We should live lives in constant gratitude to the One that has forgiven us much. But do we?

Nope.

PHIL 2:1-4

¹So if there is any encouragement in Christ, any comfort from love, any participation in the Spirit, any affection and sympathy, ²complete my joy by being of the same mind, having the same love, being in full accord and of one mind. ³Do nothing from rivalry or conceit, but in humility count others more significant than yourselves. ⁴Let each of you look not only to his own interests, but also to the interests of others.

LUKE 1:39-48

³⁹In those days Mary arose and went with haste into the hill country, to a town in Judah, ⁴⁰and she entered the house of Zechariah and greeted Elizabeth. ⁴¹And when Elizabeth heard the greeting of Mary, the baby leaped in her womb. And Elizabeth was filled with the Holy Spirit, ⁴²and she exclaimed with a loud cry, "Blessed are you among women, and blessed is the fruit of your womb! ⁴³And why is this granted to me that the mother of my Lord should come to me? ⁴⁴For behold, when the sound of your greeting came to my ears, the baby in my womb leaped for joy. ⁴⁵And blessed is she who believed that there would be a fulfillment of what was spoken to her from the Lord."

⁴⁶And Mary said;
  "My soul magnifies the Lord,
⁴⁷and my spirit rejoices in God my Savior,
⁴⁸for he has looked on the humble estate of his servant.

LUKE 1:49-55

For behold, from now on all generations will call me
blessed;
[49]for he who is mighty has done great things for me,
and holy is his name.
[50]And his mercy is for those who fear him
from generation to generation.
[51]He has shown strength with his arm;
he has scattered the proud in the thoughts of their hearts;
[52]he has brought down the mighty from their thrones
and exalted those of humble estate;
[53]he has filled the hungry with good things,
and the rich he has sent away empty.
[54]He has helped his servant Israel,
in remembrance of his mercy,
[55]as he spoke to our fathers,
to Abraham and to his offspring forever."

DISCUSSION QUESTIONS

1. *(Per the DVD)* Read Mary's song in Luke 1, paying close attention to how he handles the meek and lowly. Are pride and a sense of entitlement in your life?

_____

_____

_____

_____

_____

2. How can you, like Mary, say that your soul 'magnifies the Lord' (Luke 1:46)?

_____

_____

_____

_____

_____

3. Mary sang this after receiving great news. How can we do that after we have just heard dreadful news or, really, news of any kind?

_____

_____

_____

_____

_____

4. How is it that we have managed to kill gratitude in our lives? Why do we feel a sense of entitlement instead of thankfulness?

_____

_____

_____

_____

_____

5. Are you around meek people? Who? Are you sensitive to desiring to emulate them as you interact with them, or do you admire them and leave their presence as the same person ('that's great, that's how *they* are')?

_____

_____

_____

_____

_____

_____

_____

THE IDEA PRESENT IN CHAPTER 2 IS SO EVER-PRESENT IN THE SCRIPTURES, THAT I WOULD SAY THAT IF YOU TRY AND WRING THE SCRIPTURES OUT, IT'S WHAT WOULD COME OUT.

6. What are the effects on a community of believers when Philippians 2:2 is followed or ignored?

_____

_____

_____

_____

_____

_____

_____

HIS MERCY IS ON THOSE WHO FEAR HIM.

7. Philippians 2:3 says to do *nothing* out of rivalry or conceit. Is that realistic?

_____

_____

_____

_____

_____

_____

_____

IT IS A RARE OCCURRENCE IN THE SCRIPTURE TO SEE GOD TAKE A STRONG, CAPABLE, BRILLIANT, POWERFUL MAN AND EXALT HIM IN ANY TYPE OF REAL WAY. INSTEAD, HE CHOOSES TO USE NOBODIES.

8. We can learn a lot about what the Scriptures *do* say by what they *do not* say. 2:3 DOES say: 'in humility *count* others more significant than yourselves'. Does NOT say: '*treat* others more significant than yourselves'. What if it said the latter, not the former? What would the implication be?

_____

_____

_____

_____

_____

_____

_____

9. We are called to have confidence in Christ (2 Cor 3:4; Eph 3:12; Heb 3:5-6; 4:16). How do you 'fear' God while approaching with confidence?

_____

_____

_____

_____

_____

_____

_____

_____

10. Summarize the teaching of this passage in one sentence.

_____

_____

_____

_____

_____

_____

_____

memory verse

Do nothing from rivalry or conceit, but in humility count others more significant than yourselves. (Philippians 2:3, ESV)

DIVING DEEPER

There is a close Old Testament parallel to Mary's song in the New Testament. It is the song of Hannah in 1 Samuel 2:1-10. Read this incredible passage of another woman magnifying the Lord upon hearing the news that she will in fact have a child. The setup is 1 Samuel 1, and the song of response is chapter 2.

Read Philippians 2:6-11 in different translations to see how different translators have interpreted the Greek.

prayer requests

_____

_____

_____

_____

_____

_____

_____

_____

_____

THE ONE GOD OPPOSES 4

PHILIPPIANS 2:3-11, LUKE 1:50-53

I had a buddy in college that everyone wanted to be around. He was incredibly positive, always upbeat, and never having a bad day—so it seemed. He was so constantly happy, I can literally recount in my mind scores of people that always wanted to be around him. He, by being joyful and positive, was a ray of light when people were having a bad day, and it was contagious. I bought into the fact that, yes, I could in fact spend every waking minute with this guy. It seemed that this quality of amazing, constant joy was one that was attractive and there is never a time that anyone would not want to be with someone that possessed this trait.

I was wrong.

After a while, I found that there were in fact many instances where grief was appropriate and his demeanor did not change one bit. He still tried to find the positive and bring the group up. His energy and excited spirit that had been so attractive for so long was now downright annoying. I started out singing his praises, and by the end of my four years, literally wanted to beat him. Maybe incredible joy is not a quality in an individual that automatically endears everyone to you after all. Perhaps you can have 'enough' joy.

But there are qualities that one can never have enough of. I would argue that one such quality is wisdom. Read Proverbs sometime and bask in the way that wisdom is exalted. Look at how it praises those that seek it and constantly grow in it. One can never have enough, and one with wisdom always seems to have people around. I have never been annoyed by anyone with so much wisdom. (If they flaunted how much they had it was arrogance, and therefore not wisdom.) They are desirous to others, no matter how much they have. In fact, the more they have, the more people tend to flock to them.

There is at least one other quality that seems to constantly attract others and never is complained about. It seems that one can never get enough of it, and never be complained about having too much. It is also the first part of what Paul writes about in Philippians 2.

Complete, utter *humility*. I didn't really need this session because I am so incredibly awesome at being humble (I mean seriously—the best ever!), but I assume you might need to hear it.

PHIL 2:3-11

3Do nothing from rivalry or conceit, but in humility count others more significant than yourselves. 4Let each of you look not only to his own interests, but also to the interests of others. 5Have this mind among yourselves, which is yours in Christ Jesus, 6who, though he was in the form of God, did not count equality with God a thing to be grasped, 7but made himself nothing, taking the form of a servant, being born in the likeness of men. 8And being found in human form, he humbled himself by becoming obedient to the point of death, even death on a cross. 9Therefore God has highly exalted him and bestowed on him the name that is above every name, 10so that at the name of Jesus every knee should bow, in heaven and on earth and under the earth, 11and every tongue confess that Jesus Christ is Lord, to the glory of God the Father.

LUKE 1:50-53

51He has shown strength with his arm;
  he has scattered the proud in the thoughts of their
  hearts;
52he has brought down the mighty from their thrones
  and exalted those of humble estate;
53he has filled the hungry with good things,
  and the rich he has sent away empty.

DISCUSSION QUESTIONS

1. *(Per the DVD)* Do you see people like they have souls or are they your servants?

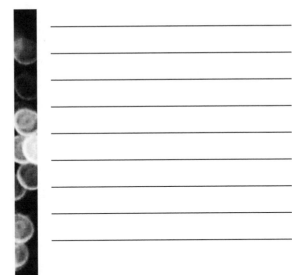

_____

_____

_____

_____

_____

_____

_____

_____

_____

_____

THE REASON THE RICH GO AWAY EMPTY IS BECAUSE THEY ARE CONSTANTLY WANTING MORE OF WHAT WILL NEVER FILL THEM.

2. *(Per the DVD)* What things can you do that aren't so pleasant so others do not have to?

_____

_____

_____

_____

_____

_____

_____

_____

_____

_____

3. What do you do when you see people chasing what appears to have value, meaning, and substance but is really chasing the wind? What do you chase that diverts your attention from God?

_____
_____
_____
_____
_____
_____
_____
_____
_____

ARE YOU USING GOD TO GET SOMETHING FROM HIM OR IS GOD THE GOAL?

4. Why do we chase wind?

_____
_____
_____
_____
_____
_____
_____
_____

THE FOUNDATION, THE MOTIVATION OF A LIFE OF HUMILITY, IS THE EXAMPLE OF JESUS CHRIST IN LIFE, AND ON THE CROSS.

5. **James 4:6** says that God 'opposes the proud and gives grace to the humble'. So?

_____

_____

_____

_____

_____

_____

_____

_____

6. Talk about the true source of our grumbling. Is it even feasible to never grumble?

_____

_____

_____

_____

_____

_____

_____

7. For who or what would you risk your life? Would you honestly be willing to lose your life so that the gospel would advance?

_____

_____

_____

_____

_____

_____

_____

8. Do you approach your community of faith with the attitude and the heart of 'how do I serve' or 'how can I be served'? How can you either become a person that approaches it to serve or stay that way if you already are?

_____
_____
_____
_____
_____
_____
_____
_____

9. An objective evidence of conversion is humility in service. What are some others?

_____
_____
_____
_____
_____
_____
_____
_____

10. Summarize the teaching of this passage in one sentence.

_____
_____
_____
_____
_____
_____
_____

DIVING DEEPER

The word translated 'imagination' in Luke 1:51 is the Greek word: διάνοια [/dee•an•oy•ah/] is comprised of two Greek words:

1) διά [/dee•ah/] is a preposition, meaning 'by', 'through', 'with', or 'for the sake of'.
2) νοια [an•oy•ah]., which means unreason or folly, and has been used in some ancient literature to describe dementia.

This phrase literally says that "He has scattered the proud in the dementia of their hearts"!

JUST IN CASE...

Scriptures on grumbling as mentioned in the DVD:

> **Proverbs 6:16-17**
> **Proverbs 8:13**
> **Proverbs 16:5**
> **James 4:6**

prayer requests

_____

_____

_____

_____

_____

NOTES

CHRISTIANITY MADE SIMPLE 5

PHILIPPIANS 3:1-9, PSALM 63

Let's get one thing straight: I am not a 'gamer'. In fact I am absolutely terrible at video games and computer games.

I am not trying to be humble in saying that. I am just... awful.

Here is the root of the problem: I quit playing them in about 5th grade, so you can imagine when I got to college how out of the loop I was. My sophomore year, I walked into my dorm and met my new roommate. He asked me if I wanted to play a video game with him. Wasn't sure what a "Sega" was, but wanting to make a good impression, I agreed. Before the inevitable slaughter could ensue, I looked at the controller in disbelief. Since I had been out of the game for quite some time, imagine my surprise when I saw a controller with more joysticks/thumbpads than I had hands and more buttons than I had fingers. Literally, I almost dropped the controller a number of times as it surprisingly shook when I got tackled. (I thought I had broken it.)

Understand my perspective. I grew up on the Atari 2600. One joystick: one button. Greatness. Learning how to play was easy. If you wanted to move the guy on the field, you move the one joystick. If you wanted to make him do... well... anything, you push the only button that is available to you. One button and one joystick sure made things easy.

When you think of the Christian life, do you think of a complicated, newfangled controller with 12 joysticks and 57 buttons? It seems complicated if we see our faith as a list of do's and don'ts, doesn't it?

Good news: Gimme that complex controller! Here is your very own Atari Joystick.

Get ready to get simple.

PHIL 3:1-9

¹*Finally, my brothers, rejoice in the Lord. To write the same things to you is no trouble to me and is safe for you.*

²*Look out for the dogs, look out for the evildoers, look out for those who mutilate the flesh. ³For we are the circumcision, who worship by the Spirit of God and glory in Christ Jesus and put no confidence in the flesh— ⁴though I myself have reason for confidence in the flesh also. If anyone else thinks he has reason for confidence in the flesh, I have more: ⁵circumcised on the eighth day, of the people of Israel, of the tribe of Benjamin, a Hebrew of Hebrews; as to the law, a Pharisee; ⁶as to zeal, a persecutor of the church; as to righteousness under the law, blameless. ⁷But whatever gain I had, I counted as loss for the sake of Christ. ⁸Indeed, I count everything as loss because of the surpassing worth of knowing Christ Jesus my Lord. For his sake I have suffered the loss of all things and count them as rubbish, in order that I may gain Christ ⁹and be found in him, not having a righteousness of my own that comes from the law, but that which comes through faith in Christ, the righteousness from God that depends on faith—*

PSALM 63:1-4

¹*O God, you are my God; earnestly I seek you;*
my soul thirsts for you;
my flesh faints for you,
as in a dry and weary land where there is no water.
²*So I have looked upon you in the sanctuary,*
beholding your power and glory.
³*Because your steadfast love is better than life,*
my lips will praise you.
⁴*So I will bless you as long as I live;*
in your name I will lift up my hands.

PSALM 63:5-11

[5]My soul will be satisfied as with fat and rich food,
   and my mouth will praise you with joyful lips,
[6]when I remember you upon my bed,
   and meditate on you in the watches of the night;
[7]for you have been my help,
   and in the shadow of your wings I will sing for joy.
[8]My soul clings to you;
   your right hand upholds me.
[9]But those who seek to destroy my life
   shall go down into the depths of the earth;
[10]they shall be given over to the power of the sword;
   they shall be a portion for jackals.
[11]But the king shall rejoice in God;
   all who swear by him shall exult,
   for the mouths of liars will be stopped.

DISCUSSION QUESTIONS

1. *(Per the DVD)* Why don't we yearn? Why is there a gap between certain 'great' men and women, and us? Is there a gap in you?

_____

_____

_____

_____

_____

_____

_____

_____

2. Why are we so easily satisfied?

_____

_____

_____

_____

_____

3. The goal is not to be looking good on the outside, but to have our goal be Him. What does that mean and how does a Christian accomplish that?

_____

_____

_____

_____

_____

4. What are some of the reasons we ought to go hard after Jesus?

_____

_____

_____

_____

_____

_____

_____

_____

5. What are the 'secondary pursuits' in our lives that distract us from the primary?

_____

_____

_____

_____

_____

_____

_____

THERE IS A MISUNDERSTANDING OF OUR FAITH THAT HAS PUT ALL OF THE WEIGHT ON CONVERSION WITH VERY LITTLE EXPECTATION FOR AFTERWARDS.

6. What are the things that stir your affections for Christ?

_____
_____
_____
_____
_____
_____
_____
_____
_____

7. The author of Hebrews makes the claim that there is sin, and then there are things that hinder you that are not necessarily 'sin' (Hebrews 12:1). What are the things that hinder you that are not 'sin'?

A. What are you responsible to do with those? Keep them to yourself? Share with someone else?

B. For what purpose?

_____
_____
_____

A._____
_____
_____

B._____
_____
_____
_____

PAUL IS SAYING THAT IF YOU GET ALL OF THESE THINGS, IF YOU CLEAN UP YOUR LIFE ON THE OUTSIDE AND MAKE IT LOOK LIKE THE CHRISTIAN COMMUNITY SAYS IT'S SUPPOSED TO LOOK, BUT YOU DON'T GET JESUS, YOU'VE LOST! WHO CARES?!

8. How can someone who lives their Christian life as a list of rights and wrongs, move it to a life that is consumed with Christ?

_____

_____

_____

_____

_____

_____

_____

_____

_____

_____

_____

_____

9. Summarize the teaching of this passage in one sentence.

_____

_____

_____

_____

_____

_____

_____

_____

_____

_____

_____

_____

_____

_____

_____

_____

_____

memory verse

Indeed, I count everything as loss because of the surpassing worth of knowing Christ Jesus my Lord. (Philippians 2:8a, ESV)

DIVING DEEPER

Psalm 63: Background

"The faith expressed in Psalms 61 and 62 reaches a climax in this marvelous hymn of David, written in the wilderness. It refers to a time when David, asking, was separated from the ark, the formal place of worship (2 Sam. 15:25). The psalmist satisfied the longing of his soul for worship by praising God for His loyal love even in his distress. As a result, he confidently anticipated a time of joy when his enemies would be stopped."[1]

prayer requests

_____

_____

_____

_____

_____

[1] John F. Walvoord, Roy B. Zuck and Dallas Theological Seminary, *The Bible Knowledge Commentary: An Exposition of the Scriptures* (Wheaton, IL: Victor Books, 1983-c1985), 1:839-840.

OWNED

6

PHILIPPIANS 3:7-12

I have a young daughter and I am already terrified for her. I already would hate to be a girl in our culture where everything seems to revolve around external beauty, but add to that the garbage that the media says to young girls especially. Every romance movie, every book, every magazine, all the groups in the world, and her peers make claims like this: "I love you because of how I feel when I am with you." (What about when the feelings leave?) "I love you because you treat me this way." (What if he treats you poorly once? Does love disappear?) "I love you because we never fight." (Then you are not in much of a relationship or someone is lying.)

What is love?

I try to express the truth of what love is to my daughter every chance I get. I remember one time I told her how much I love her before bed and a thought occurred to me. Did she know why I loved her? I told her how much I loved her. She looked at me and said she loves me, too.

I asked, "Do you know why I love you?"

She was perplexed. I can imagine that what was running through her mind was because we had fun together, because she had made some good choices that day, or because we read books together. She could not crystallize her thoughts but I could see her mind racing. Though she wanted desperately to answer she couldn't. I will never forget taking her little face in my hands and watching her look up at me with her adorable eyes that make me melt. And I told her, "I love you, because you are mine."

Isn't it nice when someone's love for you is simply because you are theirs?

Such is the love of God.

⁷But whatever gain I had, I counted as loss for the sake of Christ. ⁸Indeed, I count everything as loss because of the surpassing worth of knowing Christ Jesus my Lord. For his sake I have suffered the loss of all things and count them as rubbish, in order that I may gain Christ ⁹and be found in him, not having a righteousness of my own that comes from the law, but that which comes through faith in Christ, the righteousness from God that depends on faith— ¹⁰that I may know him and the power of his resurrection, and may share his sufferings, becoming like him in his death, ¹¹that by any means possible I may attain the resurrection from the dead.

¹²Not that I have already obtained this or am already perfect, but I press on to make it my own, because Christ Jesus has made me his own.

DISCUSSION QUESTIONS

1. *(Per the DVD)* What is it that stirs your affections for Jesus Christ, and what is it that robs those affections?

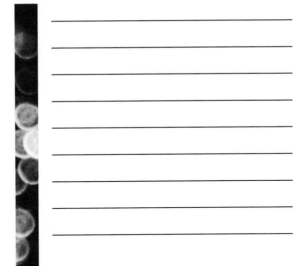

_____

_____

_____

_____

_____

_____

_____

_____

THERE HAD BETTER BE PROGRESSIVE SANCTIFICATION. THERE HAD BETTER BE GROWTH. THERE HAD BETTER NOT BE INDIFFERENCE...TO BE INDIFFERENT TO CHRIST IS A PLACE WHERE YOU NEED TO BE CONCERNED.

2. What are the three reasons that Paul gives to pursue Christ?

A._____

_____

B._____

_____

C._____

_____

3. True or false: The church where everyone looks pretty on the outside is dangerous. Explain:

_____
_____
_____
_____
_____
_____
_____
_____
_____

4. It seems that when Christians fall into great sin they retreat. They retreat from God, their spouse, their friends, and their God. Why is that? What would you tell someone that might help them learn to move towards God and his people instead of away during those times?

_____
_____
_____
_____
_____
_____
_____
_____
_____
_____
_____
_____

HOW DO YOU BEAT SIN? PRESSING INTO JESUS.

5. Why don't we yearn for God?

_____

_____

_____

_____

_____

_____

_____

_____

6. Church as a 'hobby' is a terrible way to live your life. What is an appropriate word for filling in the blank? "Church is a _____".

_____

_____

_____

_____

_____

_____

_____

_____

7. What exactly is the help to Christians today to see the men and women in the Bible and all throughout Christian history living deeply for Christ?

A. What can you do to let that impact you in a greater way?

_____

_____

_____

_____

A._____

_____

_____

_____

8. One of the main challenges of this text is to move things you value that are ridiculous and think of them as rubbish. That means moving them from things that may have driven you for years to completely moving them out of your life. How does that happen?

_____

_____

_____

_____

_____

_____

_____

_____

_____

_____

_____

_____

9. Summarize the teaching of this passage in one sentence.

_____

_____

_____

_____

_____

_____

_____

GOD RESCUES THE DIRTY TO THE PRAISE OF HIS GLORIOUS GRACE.

memory verse

Indeed, I count everything as loss because of the surpassing worth of knowing Christ Jesus my Lord. For his sake I have suffered the loss of all things and count them as rubbish, in order that I may gain Christ and be found in him, not having a righteousness of my own that comes from the law, but that which comes through faith in Christ, the righteousness from God that depends on faith. (Philippians 3:8-9, ESV)

DIVING DEEPER

Definitions:

> *Justification:* "A forensic term, opposed to condemnation…the judicial act of God, by which He pardons all the sins of those who believe in Christ, and accounts, accepts, and treats them as righteous in the eye of the law, i.e., as conformed to all its demands". Synonyms for Justification are: regeneration and conversion.

> *Sanctification:* "The carrying on to perfection the work begun in regeneration, and it extends to the whole man".

Justification is a singular point in time, sanctification is a process.

prayer requests

_____

_____

_____

_____

_____

_____

_____

_____

NOTES

NEVER SATISFIED

PHILIPPIANS 3:12-15

SCENE: *Interior. Major airport in the continental US.*

"Excuse me, we are not from around here."

"Can I help you find something?"

"We are looking for a place to eat. Preferably some good Mexican food."

"No problem. I know the perfect place. Exit the airport and drive a little bit. You will see it eventually out the window."

(Awkward pause.) "Um… can you be more specific?"

"No."

(Even more awkward pause.)

"No need to thank me."

"I won't."

Isn't this a ridiculous scene? The person would never just say, 'go' giving that vague of direction to someone in need. Yet in our faith, pastors stand up all the time and say things like, 'go live for Christ', 'grow in your faith', and 'become more like Jesus'.

Vagueness really does us no good.

Let's get specific.

PHIL 3:12-15

¹²Not that I have already obtained this or am already perfect, but I press on to make it my own, because Christ Jesus has made me his own. ¹³Brothers, I do not consider that I have made it my own. But one thing I do: forgetting what lies behind and straining forward to what lies ahead, ¹⁴I press on toward the goal for the prize of the upward call of God in Christ Jesus. ¹⁵Let those of us who are mature think this way, and if in anything you think otherwise, God will reveal that also to you.

DISCUSSION QUESTIONS

1. *(Per the DVD)* What are some spiritual goals that you might need to set for yourself? Remember, these need to be tangible, possible, and need to have some kind of time frame attached to them.

_____

_____

_____

_____

_____

_____

_____

_____

_____

YOU CAN ALWAYS FIND PEOPLE THAT YOU CAN GET AROUND AND COME ACROSS LIKE A SPIRITUAL GOLIATH. IT IS BETTER TO CONSTANTLY MEASURE YOURSELF AGAINST THE HOLINESS AND PERFECTION OF CHRIST.

2. What changes would need to take place for someone to become an applier of the Scriptures instead of just one who acquires more knowledge of it?

_____

_____

_____

_____

_____

_____

_____

_____

_____

3. How do you develop a holy discontentment? What things are OK to be discontent about, and are there things that are not?

_____

_____

_____

_____

_____

_____

_____

_____

THE VICTORY OF YESTERDAY WAS GIVEN TO US BY THE GRACE OF YESTERDAY. THE VICTORY OF TODAY WILL BE GIVEN TO YOU BY THE GRACE OF TODAY.

4. If knowing where you are weak and where you are strong serves as the basis for holy discontentment, where are you weak and strong? Who are others you can ask to help you see this in you?

_____

_____

_____

_____

_____

_____

_____

NOBODY STUMBLES INTO GODLINESS. EVER.

5. Who are some men and women that are weak where you are strong? How can you purposely sharpen each other?

_____
_____
_____
_____
_____
_____
_____
_____

6. What are some of your 'victories' in your past?

_____
_____

A. Are you remembering them in a positive way (encouragement) or negative way (complacency)?

A._____
_____
_____

7. List some other areas of life in which you strain (i.e. job, school, etc.)? Why do those come to the surface and take priority over spiritual straining?

_____
_____
_____
_____
_____
_____
_____

8. Summarize the teaching of this passage in one sentence.

_____
_____
_____
_____
_____
_____
_____
_____
_____
_____

memory verse

I press on toward the goal for the prize of the upward call of God in Christ Jesus. (Philippians 3:14, ESV)

JUST IN CASE...

Here are the 2 other Scriptures quoted in the video with regards to straining towards Christ:

1 Timothy 4:7-10
1 Corinthians 9:24

prayer requests

_____
_____
_____
_____
_____
_____

WAITING 8

PHILIPPIANS 3:16-21, TITUS 2:1-8

I truly love traveling internationally. It reminds me that there is a lost and dying world that desperately needs Jesus. It introduces me to more cultures, and affords me so many experiences that I would never get staying here in the States. But it teaches me something else each time, especially when I go to a foreign country. It is frustrating not getting American TV channels, for sure, and the language is usually a pretty good barrier, but it goes much deeper than that. I have been to countries that rock my world.

Let me describe them to you. I am talking about countries where:
... if you get caught by the government you might literally be killed.
... you can't flush toilet paper because it will clog the toilet.
... you have to keep your mouth completely sealed shut in the shower because if any of the water gets in your mouth you will be out of commission for the rest of the trip.
... electricity? Yeah right.
... there is almost no food that I can eat in the entire country without getting sick.

I would NEVER choose to live long-term in those situations. How in the world do I make it through week-long trips in those horrid circumstances for my spoiled Americans tastes? How can my weak American self make it in those circumstances?

Simple: I know it is temporary.

I know that one day soon—I am headed home.

How can I live the Christian life? Simple: This life is temporary. It stinks some days, but I know that some day—I am headed home.

What do I do in the mean time?

PHIL 3:16-21

[16]Only let us hold true to what we have attained.

[17]Brothers, join in imitating me, and keep your eyes on those who walk according to the example you have in us. [18]For many, of whom I have often told you and now tell you even with tears, walk as enemies of the cross of Christ. [19]Their end is destruction, their god is their belly, and they glory in their shame, with minds set on earthly things. [20]But our citizenship is in heaven, and from it we await a Savior, the Lord Jesus Christ, [21]who will transform our lowly body to be like his glorious body, by the power that enables him even to subject all things to himself.

TITUS 2:1-8

[1]But as for you, teach what accords with sound doctrine. [2]Older men are to be sober-minded, dignified, self-controlled, sound in faith, in love, and in steadfastness. [3]Older women likewise are to be reverent in behavior, not slanderers or slaves to much wine. They are to teach what is good, [4]and so train the young women to love their husbands and children, [5]to be self-controlled, pure, working at home, kind, and submissive to their own husbands, that the word of God may not be reviled. [6]Likewise, urge the younger men to be self-controlled. [7]Show yourself in all respects to be a model of good works, and in your teaching show integrity, dignity, [8]and(sound speech that cannot be condemned, so that an opponent may be put to shame, having nothing evil to say about us.

DISCUSSION QUESTIONS

1. *(Per the DVD)* How are you going to apply the truth of God and when?

_____

_____

_____

_____

_____

_____

_____

2. *(Per the DVD)* Are you being obedient to that which you already know?

_____

_____

_____

_____

_____

_____

_____

3. *(Per the DVD)* Who are godly men and women that you can get 'under'? What keeps younger Christians from seeking out these relationships? What characteristics should these people have?

_____

_____

_____

_____

_____

_____

4. *(Per the DVD)* Where are your eyes?

_____

_____

_____

_____

_____

_____

_____

YOUR GROWING IN TRUTH IS INSEPARABLY CONNECTED TO YOUR PRACTICING OF THE TRUTH THAT YOU ALREADY KNOW.

5. Why do we always want something new as opposed to growing in what we already know?

_____

_____

_____

_____

_____

_____

_____

_____

6. In what areas are you essentially living out a lie by not applying what you know? Who could you talk through this with, confess to, and get prayer coverage from?

_____

_____

_____

_____

_____

_____

_____

_____

7. The Christian's eyes and hearts should be set on the day where all is made right and we sit at the banquet table of the Lamb. Why do we substitute this fallen, broken, pathetic world for that glorious reality? What specifically diverts our gaze?

_____

_____

_____

_____

_____

_____

_____

THERE IS CONSTANT THE IDEA IN THE NEW TESTAMENT THAT OUR FAITH, ALTHOUGH PERSONAL, WAS NEVER MEANT TO BE PRIVATE.

8. Any time something negative happens, it is a gift to remind us of our fallen, broken world." Is it really a gift? Is it truly possible to see the negative things that happen as a reminder that this is not home?

_____

_____

_____

_____

_____

_____

_____

9. Summarize the teaching of this passage in one sentence.

_____

_____

_____

_____

_____

_____

_____

memory verse

But our citizenship is in heaven, and from it we await a Savior, the Lord Jesus Christ, who will transform our lowly body to be like His glorious body, by the power that enables him even to subject all things to himself. (Philippians 3:20-21, ESV)

DIVING DEEPER

Take a few moments and read "Behind the Book" in this study guide, catching even more of the significance of Paul's quote, "our citizenship is in heaven" (Phil 3:20).

prayer requests

REJOICE?

PHILIPPIANS 4:4-6, ROMANS 11:33-36

I've always said that there are two types of people in the world: those who divide people in the world into two categories, and those that don't.

Sorry. That was stupid.

An actual smart person, Mark Twain, said, "There are basically two types of people: people who accomplish things and people who claim to have accomplished things. The first group is less crowded."

Biblically (and really practically), I would say that there truly are two distinct types of people in the world: those in the midst of hard times and those headed for them.

Which one are you?

Teaching abounds on this topic and what to do when hard times hit and what to do to prepare for the inevitable. What is the Christian to do? It is easy to say the right Christian things, but really does it help? How can we avoid Christian cheese and give actual, relevant assistance to tough times? What can we do for ourselves in hard times when our emotions are running high and we reek of desperation and pain?

The answer might be simpler than you think.

PHIL 4:4-6

⁴Rejoice in the Lord always; again I will say, Rejoice. ⁵Let your reasonableness be known to everyone. The Lord is at hand; ⁶do not be anxious about anything, but in everything by prayer and supplication with thanksgiving let your requests be made known to God.

ROM 11:33-36

³³Oh, the depth of the riches and wisdom and knowledge of God! How unsearchable are his judgments and how inscrutable his ways!
³⁴"For who has known the mind of the Lord,
    or who has been his counselor?"
³⁵"Or who has given a gift to him
    that he might be repaid?"
³⁶For from him and through him and to him are all things.
    To him be glory forever. Amen.

DISCUSSION QUESTIONS

1. *(Per the DVD)* What situations have you been in, what tragedies have befallen you, that you would ask God to redeem? What can you dwell on now that might change your perspective, knowing the teaching of this text?

WHY DO THE MATURE REJOICE IN THE LORD ALWAYS, AND AGAIN I SAY, 'REJOICE'? BECAUSE WE CAN BE REASONABLE IN THE MIDST OF WHATEVER SITUATION BECAUSE THE LORD IS AT HAND.

2. 'God knows every fact. Ever.' What are the implications of that in your life? What about as you plan your life—mate, kids, jobs, money, etc.

3. 'He does not owe you anything.' What does that imply when struggles and hard times hit?

_____

_____

_____

_____

_____

_____

_____

THERE IS NOTHING ANYWHERE IN THE UNIVERSE THAT HE DOESN'T RIGHTLY STAND OVER, REIGN OVER, AND RIGHTLY PROCLAIM, 'MINE'.

4. *(Per the DVD)* Matt describes his child as something 'on loan from God' and 'everything I have is already His'. Do you see your kids like that? Your job like that? Your spouse? Your money?

A. How would your life change in these areas if you truly saw it that way?

A._____

_____

_____

_____

5. The session talks about not scrutinizing God. We probably do not do that overtly, but are there subtle ways we live where we show a lack of faith and arrogance by scrutinizing Him?

_____

_____

_____

_____

_____

_____

6. What does a person look like who is rejoicing biblically? Smiling? Energetic? Weeping?

_____

_____

_____

_____

_____

_____

_____

YOU WILL NOT PUT GOD IN YOUR DEBT. HE DOES NOT OWE YOU ANYTHING.

7. One of the toughest things is when we see someone hurting to give wise counsel. We give either ridiculous Christian advice ("Smile... God is in control."), or go the other extreme and do them injustice ("I understand. It is OK to be mad and to be frustrated with God"). What can you tell a person who is hurting? A way to think about it might be to ask yourself what could someone say to you that would actually help?

_____

_____

_____

_____

_____

_____

_____

8. Summarize the teaching of this passage in one sentence.

_____

_____

_____

_____

_____

_____

_____

memory verse

Rejoice in the Lord always; again I will say, Rejoice. (Philippians 4:4, ESV)

prayer requests

MATURE FAITH

PHILIPPIANS 4:4-10

Anyone with children knows that there is a beauty in the innocence and naïveté of a child. When a child is born and helpless, a mom and dad grin ear-to-ear in joy, yet in the same instant feel the awesome weight of the truth that this kid can do nothing on his own. He is helpless without the parents.

As children grow a bit, they are weaned and begin to use a bottle to get their food. It is perfectly natural for a 1 year-old to take a bottle. But can you imagine if I had been speaking in this DVD and suddenly reached down and taken a sip of coffee, *out of a baby bottle*? How ridiculous! A grown man has no business taking a bottle—those are for infants.

There are things that as you grow in your life you leave behind. You leave behind diapers, a bottle, a crib, and all sorts of toys for toddlers and babies. As a maturing believer, there are things to leave behind as you grow as well. Hebrews 5:11-14 talks about the believer who is immature and infantile. It is as ridiculous as a grown man drinking from a baby bottle as it is for a believer to still be at the basics when he is years into the faith. We have become, I am afraid, pretty good at covering up our inadequacies and have learned to justify that way of living. That is not God's plan for the believer.

We are not to be stagnant and stupid, but to be faithful and flourish.

But... how?

PHIL 4:4-10

4Rejoice in the Lord always; again I will say, Rejoice. 5Let your reasonableness be known to everyone. The Lord is at hand; 6do not be anxious about anything, but in everything by prayer and supplication with thanksgiving let your requests be made known to God. 7And the peace of God, which surpasses all understanding, will guard your hearts and your minds in Christ Jesus.

8Finally, brothers, whatever is true, whatever is honorable, whatever is just, whatever is pure, whatever is lovely, whatever is commendable, if there is any excellence, if there is anything worthy of praise, think about these things. 9What you have learned and received and heard and seen in me— practice these things, and the God of peace will be with you.

10I rejoiced in the Lord greatly that now at length you have revived your concern for me. You were indeed concerned for me, but you had no opportunity.

DISCUSSION QUESTIONS

1. *(Per the DVD)* What is going on in that head of yours? Where does your mind find itself dwelling?

_____

_____

_____

_____

_____

_____

_____

_____

_____

_____

WE MUST, IN OUR MINDS, CONSTANTLY BE EXERCISING IN TRUTH.

2. What discipline does Paul say we use to combat anxiety? What type of that discipline is used?

_____

_____

_____

_____

_____

_____

_____

_____

3. Who are some people you know that are marked by peace?

A. What external things do you see that make you believe that about them?

B. What would you suppose is going on internally in that person?

A._____

B._____

4. Discuss the balance of truth and emotions. How can a Christian keep in tension the true doctrine of Scripture, yet keep the relational aspect alive?

5. What are some of the lies that believers buy into that pull them into sin?

6. Flesh out "dwell on truth". What does that mean? How does it look in everyday life?

_____
_____
_____
_____
_____
_____
_____

IT'S NOT NATURAL TO LAY ALL ANXIETY DOWN.

7. What is a fantasy of yours that you can call to mind regularly?

_____
_____
_____
_____
_____
_____
_____
_____

8. Summarize the teaching of this passage in one sentence.

_____
_____
_____
_____
_____
_____

memory verse

Do not be anxious about anything, but in everything by prayer and supplication with thanksgiving let your requests be made known to God.
(Philippians 4:6, ESV)

prayer requests

POLAR OPPOSITES 11

PHILIPPIANS 4:10-13

We often hear in weddings that the bride and groom will be together:
>"for better, or for worse,
> for richer or for poorer
> in sickness and in health."

That is a lovely sentiment that we even said at my wedding and I have used in several weddings I have performed.

However...

I truly believe that when I promised that to my wife, I had in the back of my mind that 'better' will be awesome and the 'worse' will never really get that bad, that we may not be *exceedingly* 'rich', but we will not ever be that 'poor' either. We might not be in perfect 'health' our whole lives, but neither of us will be that 'sick'.

I think my perspective was (and still is) that I will live my life with some nice upsides, and some minor setbacks—nothing more. I think the extreme circumstances are just that— extreme. A few might hit them, but not many.

Paul did. And when a man goes into those wild swings of extreme lows and ridiculous highs, it makes sense that we kick back and see how he handled it and what counsel he might have for us today. If he can honor Christ through all that he endured, surely we in our (usually) minor swings can keep the faith.

Right?

¹⁰I rejoiced in the Lord greatly that now at length you have revived your concern for me. You were indeed concerned for me, but you had no opportunity. ¹¹Not that I am speaking of being in need, for I have learned in whatever situation I am to be content. ¹²I know how to be brought low, and I know how to abound. In any and every circumstance, I have learned the secret of facing plenty and hunger, abundance and need. ¹³I can do all things through him who strengthens me.

DISCUSSION QUESTIONS

1. *(Per the DVD)* What part of Paul's story stood out to you? What is the benefit of knowing those events?

_____

_____

_____

_____

_____

_____

_____

_____

HOW LONELY ARE YOU IN THAT MOMENT WHEN YOU TURN YOUR LIFE OVER TO THE LORD AND ARE REJECTED BY YOUR OLD FRIENDS BUT HAVE NO NEW FRIENDS?

2. Who do you know that has the combo of life experience and wisdom?

A. Are you on a course to be that kind of person?

B. What could you do to change your trajectory to get on that path if you are not now?

_____

_____

_____

A._____

_____

_____

B._____

_____

_____

_____

_____

3. Have you ever, like Paul 'stumbled' onto a gift? What is a gift in you that God has given? Are you fully using it or only partially? What keeps you from maximizing it?

_____

_____

_____

_____

_____

_____

4. We have highs and lows throughout life. What is your gut-level response to swings when they occur?

A. Who do you approach to walk you through the highs and lows?

_____

_____

_____

A._____

_____

_____

5. Paul seemed to intentionally walk into places where lows would be experienced. These places are where he knew that when he preached. he would be punished. Why did he do that and why do we avoid those types of situations so much?

_____

_____

_____

_____

_____

_____

6. Why haven't Christians experienced the polar opposites that Paul did? Is it just 'fate'? Something in us (i.e. cowardice)?

_____

_____

_____

_____

_____

_____

7. Summarize the teaching of this passage in one sentence.

_____

_____

_____

_____

_____

_____

PAUL SAYS, ESSENTIALLY, "I HAVE BEEN BEATEN SO MANY TIMES FOR THE CROSS OF CHRIST, I DON'T KNOW HOW MANY TIMES IT'S HAPPENED!"

memory verse

Not that I am speaking of being in need, for I have learned in whatever situation I am, to be content. (Philippians 4:11, ESV)

prayer requests

POLAR OPPOSITES

TRUE CONTENTMENT 12

PHILIPPIANS 4:11-23

It is easy to become discontent. I recently heard a comedian talk about a man who got on a plane and the stewardess told him that they had wireless Internet access available. Seriously? Is it not enough that you are flying through the air in a comfy chair? The man was thrilled. Think about it: he just finds out about this—that he can surf the web while flying somewhere. Amazing! He is excited.

About 5 minutes into the flight, the Internet goes down and he gets kicked offline. He calls over the stewardess and complains unceasingly. The miracle of technology that he knew about only 5 minutes earlier is something to which he is all of a sudden greatly entitled and greatly wronged if it fails him.

His sad story is our sad story. How quickly can we get something new and it satisfies and we find contentment, yet that new thing grows old quickly.

It is amazing to me in our culture today how quickly new things become old things.

How easily we become discontent in a society that has everything.

Not Paul...

¹¹Not that I am speaking of being in need, for I have learned in whatever situation I am to be content. ¹²I know how to be brought low, and I know how to abound. In any and every circumstance, I have learned the secret of facing plenty and hunger, abundance and need. ¹³I can do all things through him who strengthens me.

¹⁴Yet it was kind of you to share my trouble. ¹⁵And you Philippians yourselves know that in the beginning of the gospel, when I left Macedonia, no church entered into partnership with me in giving and receiving, except you only. ¹⁶Even in Thessalonica you sent me help for my needs once and again. ¹⁷Not that I seek the gift, but I seek the fruit that increases to your credit. ¹⁸I have received full payment, and more. I am well supplied, having received from Epaphroditus the gifts you sent, a fragrant offering, a sacrifice acceptable and pleasing to God. ¹⁹And my God will supply every need of yours according to his riches in glory in Christ Jesus. ²⁰To our God and Father be glory forever and ever. Amen.

²¹Greet every saint in Christ Jesus. The brothers who are with me greet you. ²²All the saints greet you, especially those of Caesar's household.

²³The grace of the Lord Jesus Christ be with your spirit.

DISCUSSION QUESTIONS

1. *(Per the DVD)* How do we become someone that does not just give mental assent to facts but have our life changed by the Bible and by Christ?

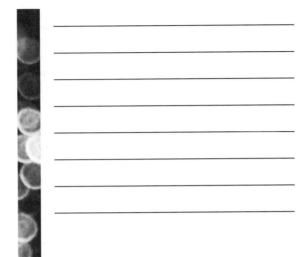

> **WE LIVE IN A WORLD WHERE THERE IS MORE TO DO THAN EVER IN THE HISTORY OF MANKIND, AND THE BULK OF US ARE BORED OUT OF OUR MINDS AND FRUSTRATED.**

2. Define 'contentment'.

3. What are the two places from which we learn contentment?

_____

_____

A. Of the two places, which do you learn more from?

_____

A._____

B. Are you exclusively from one or the other?

_____

C. Why do you think you lean towards one over the other?

B._____

_____

_____

C_____

_____

_____

IF YOU ARE HAVING TO LEARN TO BE CONTENT, THEN BEING CONTENT IS NOT NATURAL.

4. *(Per the DVD)* Matt is telling a story of his horrible illness in Asia and how he had sweet times with the Lord during that episode. *How does someone in a time like that have a sweet time with the Lord? Is that realistic for all Christians or just pastors?*

_____

_____

_____

_____

_____

_____

CONTENTMENT IS NOT IN ANY WAY RELATED TO YOUR CIRCUMSTANCES.

5. How would you explain to someone—in context—Philippians 4:13? Are there any other passages that come to mind that you hear often taken out of context?

_____

_____

_____

_____

_____

_____

6. Summarize the teaching of this passage in one sentence.

_____

_____

_____

_____

_____

_____

_____

_____

7. Summarize the teaching of the book of Philippians in one or two sentences. Write out some of the life lessons that you will take from this.

_____

_____

_____

_____

_____

_____

_____

_____

_____

_____

_____

_____

memory verse

And my God will supply every need of yours according to his riches in glory in Christ Jesus. To our God and Father be glory forever and ever. Amen. (Philippians 4:19-20, ESV)

JUST IN CASE...

Here are some of the other passages quoted in this message:

Habakkuk 3:17-19
Psalm 63:3

prayer requests

_____

_____

_____

_____

_____

_____

_____

_____

_____

_____

_____

_____

_____

_____

_____

_____

BEHIND THE BOOK PHILIPPIANS

PHILIPPIANS

INTRODUCTION

The pure *simplicity* of this great letter is one of the reasons that this is one of the most studied books of the Bible in churches today. It is so straightforward, that with virtually no knowledge of the context, the text still springs from the page and seems to easily and readily penetrate the heart of the reader. It is a letter that is simple and straightforward while being at the same time greatly profound. Despite the relevant life lessons that can be learned from this text with minimal understanding of the background, this book is one that comes incredibly to life once the context is realized.

When read quickly and taken at face value, the book speaks.

When read in context, it shouts.

THE AUTHOR

The first two words of the epistle (letter) say "Paul and Timothy", indicating that these are the two men from which the letter originates. These two co-wrote 2 Corinthians, Colossians, 1 and 2 Thessalonians (with Silvanus) and Philemon. So did they *both* write this one as well?

First, who was Timothy? Timothy was a man that truly lived up to the meaning of his name, ('honoring God' or 'worshiping God'[i]) as he and Paul sacrificed much of their lives and risked everything honoring and worshipping God by taking the gospel to numerous places, including Philippi on Paul's second missionary journey as recorded in Acts 16. Later, Paul would name Timothy the leader of the largest church he is to plant, the church at Ephesus. Entrusting his crown jewel, largest church, to Timothy gives us great insight into how greatly Paul esteemed him. Also especially important is that he trusted Timothy in this way when Timothy was just a young man (1 Timothy 4:12). He was man that traveled with Paul, was mentored by him, had two letters from Paul written to him later (1 and 2 Timothy), and was ultimately turned over to lead Paul's largest planted church at a young age. This was a great man that was used by God in many ways. Since Timothy and Paul are both included in the opening line, first blush would make one think that two men co-wrote this letter.

However, a closer look at the letter as a whole shows the author using "I", rather than "we", indicating that only one person is writing it. In addition, 2:19-24 speaks of Timothy in the third person, praising him as a great man that has served the author as a son does a father, and whom the author hopes to send as soon as possible. These verses make little sense if Timothy is an author. That the author uses "I" regularly, instead of "we", indicates that it is only one author. That person, the author, is the apostle Paul.

There is substantial *external* evidence that Paul is the author of this letter:

"The external evidence is strong. Those who quote the letter early—often specifically mentioning it as by Paul—include Ignatius, Clement of Rome, Polycarp, Irenaeus, Clement of Alexandria, and Tertullian. Both Marcion's 'canon' and the Muratorian Canon ascribe the book to Paul." [ii] The validity of Paul as the author by the early church fathers and historians is significant and overwhelming.

In addition, the *internal* evidence for Pauline authorship is strong.

"Clearly the work purports to come from him (1:1). Reference to Timothy is also significant since he was with the apostle when Philippi was evangelized (cf. Acts 16). Also the information the writer gave about himself (Phil. 3:4-6) harmonizes perfectly with Paul's life." [iii] The content indicates that it is Pauline. "Unlike Ephesians and Colossians, where historical allusions and autobiographical notations are sparse and therefore have prompted various scholars to question Pauline authorship of these two epistles, Philippians has been historically accepted as Paul's writing." [iv] "The consensus in evangelical scholarship is that this letter is absolutely Pauline. The letter claims to have been written by Paul and no serious doubt has been raised against this claim." [v] Since no valid objections have been raised and it claims to be written by Paul, the burden of proof is on the one who claims otherwise. There is no such proof.

This is a letter written by Paul. Internal and external facts, along with centuries of historical affirmation, attest to that fact.

Paul, of course, was the former murderer of Christians who was converted in Acts 9 and went on to write most of the New Testament. Paul is one that has served Christ faithfully and he sits under house arrest (more on that later) wondering if he will live or die. He is close to death, yet closer to Christ, as he claims that if he lives or dies, it does not matter—all that matters to him is Christ. He has truly not just grown *old*, but grown *up*, and grown *deep*. "Near the end of his hard and adventurous road, we find a man whose faith in Christ has not merely survived but aged with grace and wisdom, refined and as true as gold." [vi] Paul, transformed from murderer of Christians to unstoppable evangelist, stands as the quintessential example of the one fact that God can use anyone He chooses, despite the wretchedness of their past. God can use anyone, despite their flaws, and in fact, Paul stands as an example that sometimes God takes the flawed and uses them so that no one can get credit but God. God always uses flawed people: He has no other options.

Paul had previously spent some time in Philippi (Acts 16:12) and after having left had received a man named Epaphroditus (a messenger) from Philippi with contributions necessary to meet his needs. Paul sent Epaphroditus back to the Philippians with this letter.

(NOTE: There is some debate over whether or not the 'hymn' in Philippians 2:5-11 was written by Paul. For our purposes, we will acknowledge that the entire letter is inspired by the Spirit of God and therefore authoritative for teaching. It should also be noted that Paul saw fit to include it, so he is essentially affirming the doctrine therein. Whether or not it was originally penned by Paul or simply included is virtually irrelevant. It has the approval of Paul and the Spirit. Good enough for me.)

Paul is the author, Epaphroditus the messenger, but when and where was it written?

OCCASION

It is clear that Paul was in bondage when he wrote Philippians, but all do not agree which imprisonment he was experiencing when he wrote the book. To determine from where it was written, 7 things must be factored into the equation [vii]:

> 1) Paul was imprisoned while writing. (1:7, 13, 17)
> 2) He faced a trial that could lead to either his death (1:19-20; 2:17) or acquittal. (1:25; 2:24)
> 3) The location of his imprisonment included a praetorium (1:13) as well as members of Caesar's household. (4:22)
> 4) Timothy was with him. (1:1; 2:19-23)
> 5) Evangelistic efforts were still effectively conducted around him. (1:14-17)
> 6) Paul planned to visit the Philippians when acquitted. (2:24)
> 7) Several trips between Philippi and the place of imprisonment were made by various people during the course of Paul's imprisonment. (This is especially important in determining location.)

Historically, there have been three major locations put forth: Ephesus, Caesarea, and Rome.

EPHESUS:

Not many take this position, and it has come up only recently as a possibility. The main argument against this position is that the Scriptures record no imprisonment at Ephesus. Though Paul was imprisoned many times (2 Cor. 11:23), Ephesus is never mentioned. This is a minority position with virtually no support, and most scholars take one of the other two.

CAESAREA:

We know from Acts 23:33-35 that Paul was imprisoned in Caesarea, and it was certainly for a long period of time allowing for the correspondences back and forth from Philippi. Also, Paul's attack against the Jews was directed against those who were trying to kill him in both Jerusalem and Caesarea (Acts 21:37-26:32), whereas the Jews in Rome were not hostile to him (Acts 28:19). Further, the fact that the entire praetorian had heard of Paul's imprisonment for Christ (1:13) fits Caesarea as well because Paul was imprisoned in the praetorian of Herod in Caesarea (Acts 23:35).

However, this theory is not the majority view, nor is it the historical, traditional view, and is not without its problems.

First of all, in the account in Philippians, imminent death seems a very real, very near possibility (Phil 1:20-21; 2:17, especially). In Caesarea it does not appear that he was close to receiving a death sentence (Acts 23:35; 24:23). "As for Caesarea, Paul was confined there for two years, but imminent martyrdom is not suggested in the account which describes this confinement (Acts 23-24)." [viii] Besides, if it had been Caesarea, Paul (a Roman citizen) had a trump card that he could still have played: He could go to Rome and appeal to Caesar still before being executed. In Caesarea (really any place except Rome) death would not be imminent—he would have this other step he could take as a Roman citizen. This is a strong argument against it being written in Caesarea.

Scholars also note: "The notice of 'Caesar's household' (4:22) cannot without much straining of language and facts be made to apply to Caesarea." [ix] In addition, "Paul's account of his progress (1:12-26) loses all its force on this supposition (that he is writing from Caesarea). He is obviously speaking of some place of great consequence, where the gospel had received a new and remarkable development. Caesarea does not satisfy these conditions. It was after all not a very important place." [x]

The problems against the position that Caesarea is the place of origin are great.

ROME:

This is the traditional position, and most take the epistle written here and during the house arrest in Rome between about 60-63 AD. Acts 28:30 tells us that Paul had two years of imprisonment in Rome.

There are many reasons this position is strong.

The *surroundings* Paul describes as he writes this letter indicate a Roman surrounding. "In defense of this position is the fact that Paul mentions the Praetorian Guard (1:13), and he closes the epistle with these words: 'and all the rest of God's people send you greetings as well, especially those in Caesar's household.'" [xi] This fits especially well with a Roman origin.

His *circumstances* also indicate Rome. Paul's imprisonment speaks of an impending trial which would lead to his death which fits well with the Roman occasion (1:19-20; 2:17), because the next person he would face would be Caesar, and there would be no further appeal. "His reference to the palace guard (Phil. 1:13) as well as his concern about facing possible death (vv. 20-26) argue for his writing from Rome." [xii]

Besides his surroundings and circumstances, his *actions* indicate that this was Rome. He did have freedom during this imprisonment that we know of, making the writing of a letter during this time a real possibility. "All that is known of Paul's place of confinement in Rome at this time is that it was his own rented house... In this setting... although guarded constantly, Paul enjoyed great freedom to welcome visitors (Acts 28:17-30) and to preach and teach (Acts 28:31)." [xiii] "Paul was allowed considerable freedom during his two-year imprisonment in Rome. He was under house arrest, but no restrictions were put on his visitors or correspondence. So tradition favors Rome as the place from which Paul wrote (Philippians)." [xiv]

And there is external evidence as well to support Rome.

Marcion was a man born in AD 100 in Asia Minor (Sinope, a seaport on the Black Sea), who put together the first collection of the New Testament books. He did not consider the Old Testament authoritative, being replaced by the New, so what he put together, he considered the whole Bible. In his 'Bible', this 2nd century man attached prologues before each book that quickly gained wide usage. "The Pauline letters in Marcion's epistles were supplied with prologues sufficiently objective in character to have been subsequently taken over and reproduced in 'orthodox' copies of the Latin New Testament." [xv] Though the prologues are not inspired of God, it is worth seeing what this 2nd century man, not even 100 years after Paul, wrote, if anything, about the origins of this letter to the Philippians.

The prologue to the Philippians reads, "The Philippians are Macedonians. Having received the word of truth, they persevered in the faith, and did not accept false apostles. The apostle commends them, *writing to them from prison in Rome*" [xvi] (emphasis mine). This has rightly been used for centuries as strong external evidence for Paul writing from Rome.

The only real argument against the Roman imprisonment, is that the distance between Philippi and Rome is great, and some have recently argued that it is too far for all the journeys that took place between them. What journeys? Some argue for a number close to 7, But J. B. Lightfoot outlines four journeys at most are required to have taken place, though argues that two journeys are probable. The maximum (4) is outlined as follows. [xvii]

1) a messenger from Rome to Philippi—a messenger tells the Philippians of Paul's arrival in Rome
2) from Philippi to Rome—they send money to Paul via Epaphroditus (2:25; 4:18)
3) from Rome to Philippi—a messenger tells the Philippians that Epaphroditus is ill
4) from Philippi to Rome—Epaphroditus learns that the Philippians know he is ill (2:26)

Of the three main positions taken concerning which imprisonment Paul wrote this letter, Rome, the traditional position, makes the most sense and has the most scholarly acceptance by far. The only reason that anyone might question (the distance between and the number of trips that occurred) is easily explainable and certainly not compelling enough for us to waiver from the centuries of acceptance. This letter was written by Paul under house arrest in Rome in the early 60's.

RECIPIENTS

As someone who lives in America is an 'American', and one in Canada is a 'Canadian', someone who lives in Philippi is a 'Philippian'. This text is 'Paul's letter to the Church in Philippi', or 'Paul's Letter to the Philippians', or shorter: 'Philippians'. So who are these Philippians, besides inhabitants of Philippi?

A quick history lesson...

The first ancient city on the site of Philippi was "Krenides" which means 'fountains', and was located about ten miles inland from the Agean Sea. "The city appears to have been founded by Greek colonists from the island of Thasos in the early fourth century BC, and then later fortified by Philip of Macedon." [xviii] It is from Philip II of Macedon, the father of Alexander the Great, that the city derives the name 'Philippi'. "Royal coins issued after 356 BC first call the city "philippou". [xix] After Philip of Macedon took over the city and changed the name, he enlarged it greatly, as many people came to it and it underwent considerable construction. [xx] Philippi also had incredible gold and silver mines nearby which were quickly exhausted by Philip. Philippi boasted a fine school of medicine, making many to believe that this was perhaps Luke's hometown. Luke describes Philippi in Acts as "a leading city of the district of Macedonia and a Roman colony." (Acts 16:12)

The first century city was not large, probably fewer than about 10,000 people, but where they were located was key. Philippi was located on the often traveled Egnatian Way, the great northern east-west highway. It was strategically situated on this major road which connected the eastern provinces of the Roman Empire to Rome itself. Its location had it poised to be a city of great significance in the ancient world. Philippi became a leading, thriving city of Macedonia. Its crucial road system, "was a strategic foundation of Philip II...The position dominated the road system of northern Greece; hence it became the center for the battle of 42 BC in which Antony defeated...Brutus and Cassius." [xxi] In 42 BC, after this defeat, the Romans granted Philippi the highest status possible—a Roman colony.

Being a Roman colony meant that the citizens could purchase, own, or transfer property, file civil lawsuits in Roman courts, and were exempted from paying both toll and land taxes. This status as a Roman colony permeated the Philippian culture. "Their elevated status and wealth gave them not only confidence, but a pride that bordered on arrogance." [xxii] Philippi, from this moment on, was unmistakably Roman, and publicly proud of its ties to Rome. "The (Roman) colony (of Philippi) carefully maintained and groomed its image as a city loyal to the emperor's authority in both government and religion. Paul's first visit to Philippi will have impressed on him the city's emphatically *Roman* appearance and public culture, evidenced not least in the fact that the public inscriptions in the forum, on the streets and buildings of this Hellenistic-Roman town were exclusively in Latin. Not only citizenship and political loyalties were Roman, but even the form of local government was patterned on that of Rome...Citizens of Philippi were at the same time citizens of the city of Rome." [xxiii] Also, "The political atmosphere of the place is wholly Roman. Those in authority call themselves 'magistrates'. Their servants, like the attendant officers of the highest functionaries of Rome, bear the name of officers. The pride and privilege of Roman citizenship confront us at every turn." [xxiv] "It remains significant that when Paul wrote Philippians, the citizenship, language, culture and religion of Rome had been the city's dominant public frame of reference for over a century." [xxv] Think now of what it means when Paul tells this church that could easily find its comfort, security, and sense of self worth in having Roman citizenship, and tells them 'our citizenship is in heaven' (Phil. 3:20). Despite any urge from within them, or any external pressures in the society, they are to identify first and foremost with God, not Rome.

Acts 16:9 records the story of a man that appears to Paul in a vision and asks him to come over to Macedonia. Paul set sail with Timothy, Luke and Silas, landed in Macedonia, and journeyed inland to Philippi. On this, his second missionary journey Paul visited Philippi, and through his ministry there several people trusted Christ as their Savior (Acts 16:14-34).

Philippi, in northern Greece, was the first church established by Paul in Europe. Not unimportantly, this was the first church ever in all of Europe! "A denomination's 'first church' in any town or city has special prestige in the eyes of its adherents. Imagine then, the importance of the first known church-before there were any denominations-not merely in a single town, but in all of Europe! Such was the congregation at Philippi, in ancient Macedonia (northern Greece)." [xxvi] It was founded in AD 50 (Acts 16:12-40).

The people were predominantly Gentile. Paul and company would generally go to new cities and preach in synagogues. "So on their first Sabbath in Philippi, they probably looked for a synagogue. Instead they found a group of women who were outside the city on the banks of a river. The fact that Philippi had no synagogues indicates that there were few Jews in the city." [xxvii] "...the congregation consisted mainly of Gentiles and Paul saw them as the real future of the church. They were poor, but the fruits of faith were abundant." [xxviii]

As far as the actual church itself is concerned, "the letter reveals a church taking its share of suffering (1:29), and in some danger of division (1:27; 2:2). There may have been some leaning to a doctrine of perfectionism (3:12-13). But this letter was written to encourage progress rather than solve problems... Paul loved this church and rejoiced over its progress." [xxix]

This is a church that Paul planted, loves dearly, is strategically situated, is primarily Gentile, and takes great pride in its relationship to Rome.

AUTHENTICITY

There is very little debate that it is authentic and should be included into the canon of Scripture. "Paul's epistle to the Philippians appears in the oldest extant lists of books in the New Testament canon. It appears in the Muratorian Canon (late-second century), as well as in the canon created by Marcion (ca AD 160). Thereafter, Philippians appears in all the major New Testament canons, such as those indicated by Eusebius in his Eccelesiastical History, Athanasius of Alexandria in his Festal Letter (AD 367), and the Council of Carthage (AD 397)." [xxx]

PURPOSE

There are three reasons that have been given for writing this letter.

First, Paul has something about which he needs to *exhort* the congregation. Paul has some practical instruction for them. "He wants them to have practical instruction on how to live because of his great care for them. Though many exhortations and challenges are given, one major theme or emphasis pervades the book. All the teachings are expressions or ramifications of this one central truth. This theme is 'living the Christian life.'" [xxxi] He tells them to not worry, to press on, to model Christ, and much more. This book has much to say to us today about growing and maturing in our faith and pressing in to Christ in all humility. "If anyone had the right to boast, it was Paul. Yet he continued to lay aside personal ambition and glory in order to know Christ (3:7-11) and to glorify him (3:12-14). Paul knew that Jesus had left glory to come to earth in order to live as a man and to die on the cross. Paul held up Jesus as the example to follow, urging the Philippians to humble themselves as Christ had done." [xxxii] Paul exhorted them to follow the example of Christ.

Paul also exhorts them to joy. The word for 'joy' or 'rejoice' appears 16 times in 4 chapters. This is quite striking when we consider that this is a man writing from a house arrest who might be facing imminent death.

The exhortations contained in this letter make it just as relevant today as it did to the Philippians. "Situations such as bickering among church members, living in this evil world, giving to missionaries, and finding contentment are still issues for today's Christians. In this letter, Paul provides God's wisdom and encouragement. But most importantly, he holds up Jesus' life as a model for the believer." [xxxiii]

Secondly, Paul wants to *encourage*. This is the only one of Paul's letters in which he brings up no negative remarks for the recipients. He does not feel the need to call them to repentance, as he does the Romans, Corinthians, Ephesians, Galatians, and others, but takes the time to commend their actions. "Essentially, he wrote this letter from prison to encourage his friends in the Philippian church where he had been in prison earlier for proclaiming the gospel." [xxxiv]

Lastly, and perhaps most importantly, Paul has some things to *express*, namely his gratitude for their gift, and great love he has towards them. "The initial reason for writing, as indicated, seems to have been to thank the Philippians for their love gift." [xxxv] There was also a reason closely tied to this that is lost on us today. In Paul's day, one party would send a gift to another, then that group was obligated to send a return gift. When the return gift was received, another one must be sent back, and an endless cycle of gift-giving continues perpetually until one party excuses the other from continuing it. "He wanted to thank the Philippians for their gift (also to make sure they did not send another one, creating a cycle of gift and return-gift according to the conventions of the day.)" [xxxvi] "Even though he was in prison, facing an uncertain future, Paul wrote this thank you letter to the Philippians, a letter that expresses Paul's abundant joy in what God was accomplishing through them." [xxxvii]

This was a church he had known for a long time. "Paul had planted this church, his first church in Europe, over ten years earlier, so their friendship was longstanding." [xxxviii] Paul had known these believers for some time and his love for them ran deep. He wanted to make sure they knew how greatly he cared for them. This is his primary reason for writing them.

This letter has exhortation and encouragement, but is primarily an expression of Paul's great love for these people.

CONCLUSION

Paul had been imprisoned in Philippi, and finds himself imprisoned for the Lord once again in Rome. Let your mind soak in the fact that this letter, written under house arrest and possibly facing quick death, is generally summed up as a treatise of the joy found in Christ.

"This letter shows a man that was prepared to die and was ready to live. Both were good because both meant further relationship with Christ." [xxxix] For Paul it was all about Christ. So must it be with us.

The church had helped the apostle in numerous ways, so this epistle was written to acknowledge their help and express his appreciation and love for them.

It has been said that the whole Bible is one big love letter from God to man. Paul's letter to the Philippians is the quintessential example of a love letter written by a person to some people he loved dearly, as the primary theme of this letter is Paul's love for the Philippian church.

You could therefore argue, since this is the most loving letter in the Scriptures, the Book that is the ultimate work of love: the letter to the Philippians is the greatest expression of love that has ever been penned.

BIBLIOGRAPHY

Alexander, Pat and David. *Zondervan Handbook to the Bible.* Grand Rapids: Zondervan, 1999.

Beaumont, Mike. *Holman Illustrated Guide to the Bible.* Nashville: B & H Publishing Group, 2006.

Bockmuehl, Markus. *The Epistle to the Philppians.* Edited by Henry Chadwick. Vol. 11. Black's New Testament Commentaries. London: Hendrickson Publishers, 1998.

Bruce, F.F. *The Canon of Scripture.* Downers Grove, Il: IVP Academic, 1988.

Comfort, Philip W. *Philippians, 1-2 Thessalonians.* Vol. 16. 18 vols. Cornerstone Biblical Commentary, ed. Philip W. Comfort. Carol Stream, Il: Tyndale House Publishers, 2008.

Earle, Ralph. *The Expositor's Bible Commentary: Ephesians-Philemon.* Vol. 11. The Expositor's Bible Commentary, ed. Frank E. Gaebelein. Grand Rapids: Zondervan, 1981.

Gurtner, Daniel M. "1 Thessalonians." In *The Bible Knowledge Background Commentary: Acts-Philemon,* ed. Craig A. Evans. Colorado Springs: Victor, 2004.

Life Application New Testament Commentary. Edited by Philip W. Comfort and Dan Lins. Wheaton: Tyndale Publishers, 2001.

Lightfoot, J.B. *Philippians.* The Crossway Classic Commentaries, ed. Allister McGrath and J.I Packer. Wheaton, Il: Crossway Books, 1994.

MacDonald, William. *Believer's Bible Commentary.* Edited by Art Farstad. Nashville: Thomas Nelson Publishers, 1995.

Moo, D.A Carson and Douglas J. *An Introduction to the New Testament.* Grand Rapids: Zondervan, 2005.

Packer, J.I., Merrill C. Tenney, William White, Jr. *Nelson's Illustrated Encyclopedia of Bible Facts.* Nashville: Thomas Nelson, 1995.

Radmacher, Earl, Ronald B. Allen, and H. Wayne House, ed. *Nelson's New Illustrated Bible Commentary.* Nashville: Nelson, 1999.

Smith, Stelman and Judson Cornwall. "*The Exhaustive Dictionary of Bible Names.*" ed. Bridge-Logos. North Brunswick, NJ, 1998.

Tenney, Merrill C., ed. *Zondervan's Pictorial Bible Dictionary.* Grand Rapids: Zondervan, 1988.

Walvoord, John F., Roy B. Zuck and Dallas Theological Seminary. *The Bible Knowledge Commentary, An Exposition of the Scriptures.* Wheaton, IL: Victor Books, 1983-c1985.

i Stelman and Judson Cornwall Smith, *"The Exhaustive Dictionary of Bible Names,"* ed. Bridge-Logos (North Brunswick, NJ: 1998), 239.

ii WIlliam MacDonald, *Believer's Bible Commentary*, ed. Art Farstad (Nashville: Thomas Nelson Publishers, 1995), 1957.

iii John F. Walvoord, Roy B. Zuck and Dallas Theological Seminary, *The Bible Knowledge Commentary, An Exposition of the Scriptures* (Wheaton, IL: Victor Books, 1983-c1985), 2:647.

vi Philip W. Comfort, *Philppians, 1-2 Thessalonians*, vol. 16, 18 vols., Cornerstone Biblical Commentary, ed. Philip W. Comfort (Carol Stream, Il: Tyndale House Publishers, 2008), 142.

v D.A Carson and Douglas J. Moo, *An Introduction to the New Testament* (Grand Rapids: Zondervan, 2005), 499.

vi Markus Bockmuehl, *The Epistle to the Philppians*, ed. Henry Chadwick, vol. 11, Black's New Testament Commentaries (London: Hendrickson Publishers, 1998), 1.

vii Daniel M. Gurtner, "1 Thessalonians," in *The Bible Knowledge Background Commentary: Acts-Philemon*, ed. Craig A. Evans (Colorado Springs: Victor, 2004), 570.

viii Walvoord, *The Bible Knowledge Commentary, An Exposition of the Scriptures*, 2:647.

ix J.B Lightfoot, *Philippians*, The Crossway Classic Commentaries, ed. Allister McGrath and J.I Packer (Wheaton, Il: Crossway Books, 1994), 45.

x Ibid., 45-46.

xi Comfort, *Cornerstone Commentary: Philippians, 1/2 Thess.*, 142.

xii Walvoord, *The Bible Knowledge Commentary, An Exposition of the Scriptures*, 2:647.

xiii *Life Application New Testament Commentary*, ed. Philip W. Comfort and Dan Lins (Wheaton: Tyndale Publishers, 2001), 838.

xiv Pat and David Alexander, *Zondervan Handbook to the Bible* (Grand Rapids: Zondervan, 1999), 678.

NOTES

[xv] F.F. Bruce, *The Canon of Scripture* (Downers Grove, Il: IVP Academic, 1988), 141.

[xvi] Ibid., 142.

[xvii] Lightfoot, *Philippians*, 51.

[xviii] Bockmuehl, *The Epistle to the Philppians*, 3.

[xix] Ibid.

[xx] Ralph Earle, *The Expositor's Bible Commentary: Ephesians-Philemon*, vol. 11, The Expositor's Bible Commentary, ed. Frank E. Gaebelein (Grand Rapids: Zondervan, 1981), 95.

[xxi] Merrill C. Tenney, ed. *Zondervan's Pictorial Bible Dictionary* (Grand Rapids: Zondervan, 1988), 650.

[xxii] Earl Radmacher, Ronald B. Allen, and H. Wayne House, ed. *Nelson's New Illustrated Bible Commentary* (Nashville: Nelson, 1999), 1544.

[xxiii] Bockmuehl, *The Epistle to the Philppians*, 4.

[xxiv] Lightfoot, *Philippians*, 63.

[xxv] Bockmuehl, *The Epistle to the Philppians*, 4.

[xxvi] MacDonald, *Believer's Bible Commentary*, 1957.

[xxvii] *Life Application New Testament Commentary*, 839.

[xxviii] Tenney, ed. *Zondervan's Pictorial Bible Dictionary*, 650.

[xxix] Alexander, *Zondervan Handbook to the Bible*, 720.

[xxx] Comfort, *Cornerstone Commentary: Philippians, 1/2 Thess.*, 146.

[xxxi] Walvoord, *The Bible Knowledge Commentary, An Exposition of the Scriptures*, 2:647.

[xxxii] *Life Application New Testament Commentary*, 841.

xxxiii Radmacher, ed. *Nelson's New Illustrated Bible Commentary*, 1542-1543.

xxxiv J.I. Packer, Merrill C. Tenney, William White, Jr., *Nelson's Illustrated Encyclopedia of Bible Facts* (Nashville: Thomas Nelson, 1995), 600.

xxxv Walvoord, *The Bible Knowledge Commentary, An Exposition of the Scriptures*, 2:647.

xxxvi Alexander, *Zondervan Handbook to the Bible*, 720.

xxxvii Radmacher, ed. *Nelson's New Illustrated Bible Commentary*, 1542.

xxxviii Mike Beaumont, *Holman Illustrated Guide to the Bible* (Nashville: B & H Publishing Group, 2006), 113.

xxxix Comfort, *Cornerstone Commentary: Philippians, 1/2 Thess.*, 143.

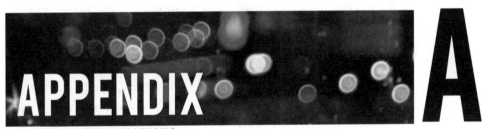

APPENDIX

ANSWER TO THE QUESTIONS

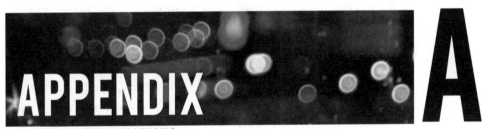

A

APPENDIX

TEXT ANSWERS – SESSION ONE

QUESTION 2

A. **Lydia (16:14-15)**
Driven, successful, intellect, seeker, god-fearer, Asian—Paul engages her intellect.

B. **The Demon-Possessed Girl (16:16-18)**
Girl with the spirit of divination = Greek, exploited and has nothing, not a seeker, manic, out of control—Paul commands the thing that ruled her/enslaved her.

C. **The Jailer (16:23-34)**
Blue-collar, ex-GI, not interested in intellects, duty-driven—Paul shows them a life lived out of duty to something higher.

TEXT ANSWERS – SESSION SIX

QUESTION 2
To work out our justification, because we are broken, He has us.

TEXT ANSWERS – SESSION TEN

QUESTION 2
prayer, supplication

TEXT ANSWERS – SESSION TWELVE

QUESTION 3
the Scriptures and experience

MATT CHANDLER

MATT CHANDLER serves as Lead Pastor of The Village Church in Dallas, TX. He describes his tenure since 2002 at The Village as a re-planting effort where he was involved in changing the theological and philosophical culture of the congregation. The church has witnessed a tremendous response growing from 160 people to over 10,000 including satellite campuses in Dallas and Denton. In March of 2012, Matt was named president of Acts 29 Network, which is a network of over 400 churches in the United States and abroad planting church-planting churches. Matt authored *The Explicit Gospel*, to remind us what is of first and utmost importance – the Gospel. It is call to true Christianity, to know the Gospel explicitly and to unite the church on the amazing grounds of the good news of Jesus.

His greatest joy outside of Jesus is being married to Lauren and being a dad to their three children, Audrey, Reid and Norah.

Two ministries that Matt would encourage you to find out more about are:

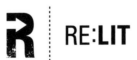

www.theresurgence.com

www.acts29network.org

Additional Resources
available by

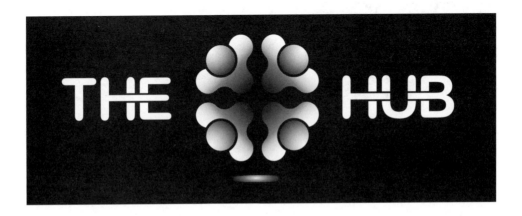

www.gotothehub.com

NEW! Ruth
A True Story of Love & Redemption
Video Teaching Series. Buy. Rent. Download.

Ruth is a courageous woman. Boaz is a generous man. Both exemplified great character. Ruth needed a redeemer. We all need a redeemer.

The Book of Ruth is simply put the greatest love story, ever. Tommy Nelson, Author, Pastor, and Teacher will lead us through this compelling story of Romance & Redemption.

In this journey you will learn:
- The Character of a Great Woman
- The Character of a Great Man
- How to Find God's Will for Life
- Your Redeemer
- Our King

About

TOMMY NELSON has been the pastor of Denton Bible Church, in Denton, Texas, since 1977. Tommy graduated from the University of North Texas with a Bachelor's Degree in Education. He then attended Dallas Theological Seminary in Dallas, Texas, where he received the Master of Arts in Biblical Studies degree.

Tommy has been married to Teresa Nelson since 1974. They have two grown sons, Ben and John, along with five grandchildren.

Study Guide recommended for each participant.

Romans, Volume I & II

The Letter that Changed the World
Video Teaching Series. Buy. Rent. Download.

The most important idea in the Bible is how a Holy God can get a sinful man into Heaven and not compromise who He is. Romans tell us just that! It sits as Master of the House before all of Paul's writings. It is the Bible in miniature. It is the most important singular document ever penned by man and only inspiration could make it so.

In our study in Romans we will look at Paul's unfolding logic and incisive reasoning as to the divinity and holiness of the Christian gospel. When this book has been understood, reformation and new life follow shortly.

Tommy Nelson

About

TOMMY NELSON has been the Pastor of Denton Bible Church, in Denton, Texas, since 1977. Tommy graduated from the University of North Texas with a Bachelor's Degree in Education. He then attended Dallas Theological Seminary in Dallas, Texas, where he received the Master of Arts in Biblical Studies degree.

Tommy has been married to Teresa since 1974. They have two grown sons, Ben and John, along with five grandchildren.

Song of Solomon 2005

Video Teaching Series. Buy. Rent. Download.

Used and loved throughout the world, the Song of Solomon series teaches the biblical design for relationships. For both singles and married couples, this study follows Solomon's relationship from attraction to dating and courtship, marriage and intimacy to resolving conflict, keeping romance alive and committing to the end. The 10th Anniversary Edition (released in 2005) updates Tommy Nelson's original study with updated teaching and added features.

SOS for Students

Video Teaching Series. Buy. Rent. Download.

Every parent, student pastor and student know the absolute need of saying, "an ounce of prevention is worth a pound of cure." God gave us the gift of love, marriage and sexuality, but since Christians have been mostly silent on this issue, many students learn these things from the secular community. As a result, students have a distorted view of sexuality and God's purpose for it.

Song of Solomon for Students teaches that God is for love and sexuality; in fact, it is His design and gift in the first place. Tommy Nelson taught these 6, 25 minute sessions to junior and senior high students. It will walk them through the first four chapters of Song of Solomon and focuses on these issues: attraction, dating and the truth about sexuality and when it is most enjoyed and most honoring to God.

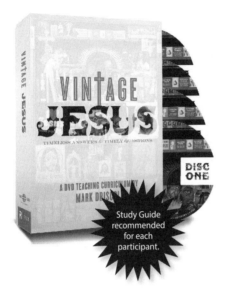

Vintage Jesus
Timeless Answers to Timely Questions
Video Teaching Series. Buy. Rent. Download.

Who do you say I am?

There is no greater question. No one is more loved and hated than Jesus. "To some an aroma of life, to others an aroma of death."

The Vintage Jesus Study Guide will drive you to the scriptures in search of Who Jesus Really Is by answering 12 of the most pressing questions about the nature, humanity and deity of our Saviour.

Author and Pastor Mark Driscoll uses humor, expertise, boldness and relevance with today's culture to help lead us to answer this question correctly.

Perhaps unlike any other Teaching Curriculum, Vintage Jesus will equip Christians to have more understanding and confidence in communicating the deity and life changing power of Jesus. For those who are seeking the Ultimate Truth of life, with relevance and grace, this series will cause everyone to think hard about Jesus' own question that He asked thousands of years ago, "Who Do You Say That I AM?"

About

PASTOR MARK DRISCOLL founded Mars Hill Church in Seattle in the fall of 1996. The church has grown from a small Bible study to upward of 13,000 people meeting weekly across 14 locations in four states, Washington, Oregon, California, and New Mexico. He co-founded Acts 29 Church Planting Network which has planted over 400 churches in the U.S., in addition to 13 other nations. He has authored *The Radical Reformission, Death by Love, Religion Saves, Doctrine* and many more.

Most of all, Mark and his high school sweetheart, Grace, enjoy raising their three sons and two daughters.

Study Guide recommended for each participant.

NEW! LoveLife
Song of Solomon
DVD Curriculum Set

What does it really mean to love? What does love look like in singleness, dating or marriage?

Through the study of Song of Solomon, Mark Driscoll reveals an Old Testament understanding of biblical sexuality with current cultural clarity.

Learn to celebrate God's gift of love in all of life by walking through this timely series.

The Mingling of Souls

A Study of Attraction, Love, Marriage & Redemption from Song of Solomon

Video Teaching Series. Buy. Rent. Download.

This teaching series looks at a document penned about 4,000 years ago that will put the most romantic, passionate individual on the planet to absolute shame. The goal is not shame, of course, but rather guidance and encouragement. Solomon is going to speak from the dead (so to speak), and give practical, helpful, biblical, time-tested guidance on how to have a thriving romantic relationship, no matter if you are married or single.

Join Matt Chandler, one of America's most listened to and influential Pastors, walk us through the Song of Solomon with his practical and funny presentation. Perfect for all of your Adult Bible Study groups and classes. Start living in God's best and redemptive love in this area of life.

About

MATT CHANDLER serves as Lead Pastor of The Village Church in Highland Village, TX. He describes his tenure at The Village as a re-planting effort where he was involved in changing the theological and philosophical culture of the congregation.

The church has witnessed a tremendous response growing from 160 people to over 8,000 including satellite campuses in Dallas and Denton. He is one of the most downloaded teachers on iTunes and consistently remains in the Top 5 of all national Religion and Spirituality Podcasts.

Matt's passion is to speak to people in America and abroad about the glory of God and beauty of Jesus.

His greatest joy outside of Jesus is being married to Lauren and being a dad to their three children, Audrey, Reid and Norah.